Putting your
in their

A Guide to One Place Studies

G000270737

Janet Few

THE FAMILY HISTORY PARTNERSHIP

Published by
The Family History Partnership
57 Bury New Road, Ramsbottom
Bury, Lancashire BL0 0BZ

www.thefamilyhistorypartnership.com

First published 2014

ISBN: 978 1 906280 43 7

Printed and bound by
Berforts Information Press
Southfield Road, Eynsham
Oxford OX29 4JB

Contents

Part One: Setting the Scene

Part 2: Sources for One Place Studies

Part 3 Pulling it All Together

Acknowledgements

Thanks are due to Martha Barnard, Roberta Boreham, Richard Ratcliffe, Stuart Raymond and Maureen Selley for their help in the preparation of this volume.

Part One
Setting the Scene

Chapter 1

The What and Why of One Place Studies

What is a One Place Study?

Our ancestors did not live in isolation. Family historians often focus on the nuclear family. Local historians concern themselves with events, buildings and famous residents. To better understand our ancestors, they need to be 'put in their place' by investigating the community of which they were a part. To bring the history of a locality to life, it should be populated with ordinary people. A One Place Study brings family and local history together, to the benefit of both fields.

A One Place Study involves dissecting a small, definable, geographical area, to examine the individuals, buildings and processes of the past, in as much detail as possible. These studies are undertaken by individuals, or groups, who have an interest in the history of a particular community, be it a parish, town, hamlet, or a single street. The researcher may live in the area, or be many miles from the heart of their study; perhaps having family associations with the location. One Place Studies differ from traditional local histories in that they focus on people, their relationship to their communities and to each other. One Place Studies are not just about indexing documents and collecting data. Ultimately they are about using that data to answer questions about a community, its residents and their lives.

There are as many different ways to conduct a One Place Study as there are people undertaking them. Elements that a One Place Study might incorporate and sources that could be used, are described in this book. It is not primarily about the sources themselves; these are explained in numerous 'how to' local and family history books, many of which are in this volume's bibliography. Although useful sources are described in the pages that follow, the emphasis is on how these records might be used. In this way, you can gain an insight into the past in your chosen community and produce a true One Place Study. A variety of possible projects are suggested. These could be carried out by individuals or small groups and a number are suitable for involving all ages. The suggestions are deliberately not very specific. Their purpose is to provide general ideas for enhancing a One Place Study, leaving the fine detail of how they might be executed up to the individual. Please do not be daunted by the long list of sources and projects. For most, a One Place Study is a hobby; an all absorbing one and one which you may well want to conduct in a professional manner but a hobby nonetheless. It is very unlikely that you will have the time or inclination to follow up all the ideas in this book and some will not be relevant to every 'place'. The aim is to suggest a range of activities that you might decide to pursue, given the opportunity.

Choosing your Boundaries

Often your boundaries choose themselves; you are doing a One Place Study because you have an existing interest in the place. Even then, you may have to decide whether your study will encompass a whole town or parish, or just a hamlet or street. There are a few things to bear in mind. Clearly, the larger and more densely populated your place, the more time your study is likely to need. Some areas are comparatively 'new', certainly in terms of human occupation. Although you might want to study earlier land use and ownership, a One Place Study of a Victorian street, will be more limited in scope than that of a parish, whose documents may date back 500 years or more. In general, older records, particularly before the mid nineteenth century, are less likely to identify precise places of residence for individuals. This means that choosing a hamlet or street, within a larger area, can create problems when it comes to linking people and places. A marriage register might tell you that John Brown was 'of this parish' but it may be very difficult to be certain whether or not he lived in your smaller 'place' within that parish.

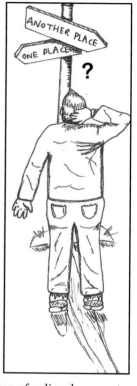

If conducting a One Place Study appeals but you do not have an affinity with a particular place, or if you are deciding between more than one place, then there are several factors to consider. If it is an option, it may be easier to choose a place that is accessible to you. Even with the recent proliferation of online documents, visiting your place on a reasonably regular basis and having relatively easy access to the relevant record repositories, is an advantage. There are still many documents that are not available online. As mentioned already, the size of the prospective places may help you to make your choice.

Something else to consider is the place name itself. Aspects of a One Place Study can be easier if the spelling of your place does not vary very much. A consistently spelt place name simplifies matters when you are searching indexes by location. For example, you may want to use a census index to identify people who were born in your place but are now living elsewhere.[1] A place name that is not likely to be misheard or mis-spelt by an enumerator who is dealing with an unfamiliar regional accent, will make life simpler. Similarly, two word place names are often problematical, as they may appear as just one of their two words. 'Buckland Brewer' in Devon, for instance,

---

[1] See Chapter 11, Tracing Migrants.

is usually spelt correctly but is often recorded as just 'Buckland', creating possible confusion with several other Bucklands in the same county. Bear in mind that, if your place name is also a common word or personal name, you will find search engines providing you with numerous spurious hits. A search for Paisley in Scotland, for example, brings up references to the place but also to the design and the former Irish politician. To a lesser extent, place names that exist in more than one country or county, such as Newport, Boston or Perth, can also create misunderstandings.[2] Before you choose your place you may also want to take into consideration the following two sections.

Has it Been Done Before?
It is preferable to study a place that is not already being researched. The Society for One-Place Studies, a very important body in this field, allows for collaboration but will only accept one registration for a place. If you are set on studying a place that has existing researchers, consider working together; see 'Group Study or One Man Band?' below. It may be that your help would be welcomed. Perhaps you can investigate the place, or an aspect of the place, in a completely new way. Ideally your work will complement, rather than duplicate, that of others.

One of the first to places to look for existing studies is under the 'Studies' listings on the website of the Society for One-Place Studies **http://one-place-studies. org/studies/**. This will tell you if your place of interest has already been claimed by one of their members. It is also a good idea to read some of the profiles and in-depth descriptions of existing studies, to get an impression of their nature, size and scope. If you decide to undertake a One Place Study, you would be well advised to join the Society for One-Place Studies. They issue an online newsletter, *Destinations*, provide publicity for your study, conduct group projects and facilitate the exchange of ideas about methodology. Their website contains many useful resources. There is also a completely separate free list, or register, of One Place Studies at **www.register-of-one-place-studies.org.uk**; it should be noted that some of the studies on this list are no longer active.

Another suggestion is to consult the Genuki website list **www.genuki.org.uk/ indexes/OPC.html** to find out if your place has an Online Parish Clerk, or OPC. Currently, counties in the south west of England are best served with OPCs. These individuals are volunteers and are not to be confused with the official, council appointed, Parish Clerks. OPCs, who may or may not also be undertaking a One Place Study, have access to transcriptions of documents relating to their parish. Typically, these will include parish registers and census returns but may go way beyond this. They offer free look-ups in the records that they hold. An OPC will not necessarily have collated or synthesised their data in any way. It might be desirable to combine a role as an OPC with a One Place Study. Note that OPCs exist for whole historic

---

[2] See Chapter 11, Tracing Migrants p. 75, for how overseas same-name places can be relevant to your research.

parishes only. If your place is a hamlet, a street within a parish, or a Victorian parish, you do not qualify as an OPC. It is, of course, possible to be a parish OPC and conduct a, more detailed, One Place Study for just part of that parish.

The website Local History Online **www.local-history.co.uk/index.html** contains a list of many local history groups. There will be additional groups, who do not feature on this list. There may also be regional listings for local history, or similar, groups for the district in which your proposed place lies. An internet search or an enquiry at the appropriate Record Office should uncover the existence of these. The British Association for Local History **www.balh.co.uk** is an umbrella organisation for local history groups. The list of groups accessed via 'Useful Links' and 'Local Societies' on their website is worth consulting, to see if your place is represented. The Community Archives and Heritage Group **www.communityarchives.org.uk** is a similar body and is free to join. It is primarily a web based organisation, which seeks to support community archives. Their website has a list of archives that have been registered with the Group. Another place to look for existing societies is Robert and Elizabeth Blatchford's *Family and Local History Handbook* (Robert Blatchford Publishing Ltd. issued periodically), see **www.genealogical.co.uk**. They also produce an Irish version.

The existence of a group, or individual researcher, focusing on your intended study area should not necessarily deter you. They may be undertaking mainstream local history research, rather than the more specialised One Place Study. You should certainly make contact, with a view to working together.

Group Study or One Man Band?
Like many other types of research, it is very unlikely that a One Place Study will ever be 'finished'. To establish a significant body of data for a larger place will take a huge time commitment, or several lifetimes. This is just one reason why you might decide to undertake a One Place Study as part of a group. Occasionally the group comes first, when a traditional local history group moves on to study the inhabitants of the area and their relationships. More frequently, a dedicated researcher will decide to seek support and form a local history society or community archive. This body may then carry out a One Place Study as a group undertaking. Collaborative studies might also arise if more than one person has a burning interest in the same place.

The obvious advantage of working together is that more can be accomplished, often by individuals taking responsibility for different aspects of the study. In addition, the establishment of a group or society helps to safeguard the future of the research. Newer and perhaps younger, researchers may stand by to take over as others are no longer able, for whatever reason.[3] For teamwork to be effective however the primary researcher and there usually is a key individual, has to be prepared to share their role as the 'expert'.

Making a Start

This book refers to many sources that can contribute to your One Place Study research. Especially for those new to One Place Studies, the range of potential data and the number of resulting projects can seem overwhelming. It is important to break down the task into manageable sections. British One Place Studies often start with transcriptions of the census returns. This makes sense as they record people, places and the relationship between them. Other sources can then be added, perhaps beginning with parish registers, land tax returns or tithe schedules.

An alternative, less common but equally valid, approach is to start not with a source but with a short time period. Then you will meet the same individuals and properties across a range of sources. You might for example, begin with the years 1901-1920, which will allow you to use such things as censuses, parish registers, the valuation office records, the war memorial and absent voters' lists.[4] Then you can gradually work backwards or forwards. The drawback of this is that you have to revisit the same sources for different date spans. This can be time consuming or impractical if you do not have easy access to the records. The advantages however may outweigh this. By concentrating on a small date span at a time you build up a comprehensive picture of your community more quickly, albeit for a limited period. This means you reach the synthesis stage, described in Part 3, much sooner. An article, exhibition or presentation about 'My Place in the Early Twentieth Century' has more popular appeal than 'My Place in the Census Returns'.

Further Reading

Coles, Alex *Choosing a Place: some practical considerations* (2011) **http://one-place-studies.org/articles/choosing-a-place-some-practical-considerations/**.

---

[3] See Chapter 12, The Future of your One Place Study, p. 84.
[4] See Chapter 5.

Chapter Two
Reconstructing the Place

Walking Your Place

It is important to get a real feel for your place. You need to understand the landscape and buildings, both residential and non-residential, of each era. Key to this is field walking. If at all possible, visit, often. Walk the streets and footpaths, study the buildings. Would the residents of a particular house have had a long, uphill walk to church? Have farm buildings been converted into dwellings? Are there former industrial buildings that are no longer being used? Is there evidence of a roof being raised, perhaps when thatch was removed? Can you see signs of two cottages being knocked into one? Physical changes can lead to demographic and occupational changes within your community, so it is really helpful if you are aware of how your place might have looked at different times.

If visiting in person is not an option, could someone make the journey on your behalf, ideally collecting photographic and video evidence for you? Alternatively, or additionally, you could take a walk round your place using the 'Street View' facility on Google Maps **maps.google.co.uk**. It is possible to use the 'print screen' function on your computer to capture screen shots in this way but please note that the resulting images are copyright and should not be published without checking the implications. The maps themselves on this site are helpful too. Google Earth **earth.google.co.uk** also enables you to use the street view function and has additional useful facilities. For example, it is possible to overlay aerial views with roads and examine static photographs of various locations.

Do not believe all you see. Older architectural styles may be mimicked by later builders. Sometimes properties will bear dates that appear to be when they were built. This is not always the case. A property owner undertaking repairs may have displayed the date of the renovations instead.

Maps

Accessing maps is a critical part of reconstructing your place. Having a series of large scale maps to annotate as you walk your place, either literally or virtually, is invaluable. Smaller scale maps will help you to set your place in the context of the surrounding area. You might consider such things as terrain, proximity to market towns and route ways, by road, rail, river and sea. It is easiest to make sense of your community if you begin with the most recent maps and work your way backwards in time, thereby gaining a better understanding of changes to your place over the years.

Ordnance Survey maps **www.ordnancesurvey.co.uk** are ideal for these purposes. The 'Old Series' of one inch to the mile maps was produced between 1805

and 1873. Reproductions of these maps are available from David and Charles, Newton Abbot, Devon TQ12 4YG **www.david-archer-maps.co.uk**. Subsequent series were begun before the first was complete. It is important to be aware that the date of the map might be some years after the actual survey was done. From 1862, six inch to the mile Ordnance Survey maps should be available; twenty five inch to the mile maps are even more useful. For some areas, maps were produced on a much larger scale. For example, Northumberland Archives hold an 1852 120 inch to the mile plan of the town of Morpeth, produced for the Local Board Of Health.[5] Alan Godfrey, Prospect Business Park, Leadgate, Consett, DH8 7PW **www.alangodfreymaps.co.uk** has published reproductions of many six inch to the mile ordnance survey maps. See also **www.cassinimaps.co.uk.**

A very important series of maps was produced between 1838 and 1854, covering three quarters of England and Wales. These were the Tithe Maps, drawn up as part of the process of reforming the tithe system. The maps do vary in quality, some surveys being more accurate than others. There were three copies of each parish map. One, for the parish, may still be held locally or will have found its way into the County Record Office. The second, bishop's, copy is usually in the Diocesan Record Office (frequently the same building as the County Record Office). The final copy, that of the Tithe Redemption Commission, is now in Class IR30 in The National Archives. As the scale of these maps is generally between thirteen and twenty six inches to the mile, they are very detailed. Be aware however that their primary purpose was to show

---

[5] Ref. NRO5789.

the boundaries of the areas owing tithes, so some maps may not record every building. Sometimes the poorer quality tithe maps resemble an irregular patchwork quilt and can be difficult to relate to the ground. Comparing road and field patterns with more recent maps will usually help with this. Tithe maps are frequently made available on microfiche and are sometimes indistinct. In this case, a solution might be to consult one of the other copies of the map, as this could be clearer.

County Record Offices and Local Studies Libraries should contain other maps that will be relevant to your study. Enclosure maps and estate maps, drawn up for individual landowners, are helpful, although these may remain in private archives. Enclosure awards, that accompanied the maps, are also useful. See The National Archives' Research Guide *Enclosure Awards* and W E Tate's *The English Village Community and the Enclosure Movements* (Gollancz 1967).

Some maps are annotated with the names of owners and occupiers. In the eighteenth and nineteenth centuries, fire insurance companies drew up a series of maps for urban districts of England and Wales. These became known as Goad maps; the name being taken from the firm that was responsible for their production from 1885. As the maps were updated at intervals, it is possible to monitor changes. The webpage **www.experian.co.uk/goad/goad-products.html** gives information about more recent Goad maps. Some of the historic Goad maps are available on CD from **digitalarchives.co.uk**. Do not overlook the maps held by The National Archives. Their Research Guides give useful background to the various types of map that they have. See also Masters, Charles *Essential Maps for Family Historians* (Countryside Books 2009).

There are several sites where facsimiles of historical maps can be purchased or downloaded. For example, **www.latitudemaps.co.uk/historicalmaps.html**, **digitalarchives.co.uk** and **www.old-maps.co.uk**.

Project - Mapping your Community

Create an historic map, or series of maps, for your place. The aim is to show all the features that may have been present at a particular point in time. For example, you could use a combination of existing maps, the 1841 census and the tithe map and schedule[6] to indicate which buildings were likely to have existed in 1841. If your study area is large, you may decide to tackle just a small part of it. Small places may only require one map, that could be coloured or annotated to indicate roughly when each current property was built. You may be able to annotate a sketch map of the buildings, as in the example for Bucks Mills shown here, or the one for Springhill **http://springhillhistory.org.uk/page20/index.html**. If you have knowledge of properties that no longer exist add these to your map. Another option is to create a series of overlays for your map, so that the appearance of your place in different eras is gradually revealed.

---

[6] See Chapter 6, p. 42.

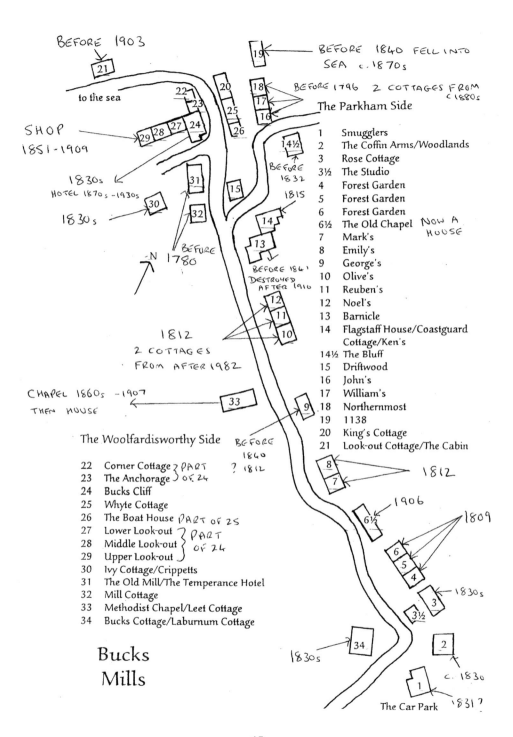

BEFORE 1903

21

to the sea

22
23

20
19 ← BEFORE 1840 FELL INTO SEA c. 1870s

18 ← BEFORE 1796 2 COTTAGES FROM c. 1880s
17
16

The Parkham Side

SHOP
1851-1909

29 28 27 24
25
26

14½
BEFORE 1832
1815

1 Smugglers
2 The Coffin Arms/Woodlands
3 Rose Cottage
3½ The Studio
4 Forest Garden
5 Forest Garden
6 Forest Garden
6½ The Old Chapel NOW A HOUSE
7 Mark's
8 Emily's
9 George's
10 Olive's
11 Reuben's
12 Noel's
13 Barnicle
14 Flagstaff House/Coastguard Cottage/Ken's
14½ The Bluff
15 Driftwood
16 John's
17 William's
18 Northernmost
19 1138
20 King's Cottage
21 Look-out Cottage/The Cabin

1830s
HOTEL 1870s - 1930s

31

30

1830s

15

32

14

13

BEFORE 1841 DESTROYED AFTER 1910

←N BEFORE 1780

12
11
10

1812
2 COTTAGES
FROM AFTER 1982

CHAPEL 1860s - 1907
THEN HOUSE

33

9

The Woolfardisworthy Side

BEFORE 1840
? 1812

22 Corner Cottage } PART OF 24
23 The Anchorage
24 Bucks Cliff
25 Whyte Cottage
26 The Boat House PART OF 25
27 Lower Look-out } PART OF 24
28 Middle Look-out
29 Upper Look-out
30 Ivy Cottage/Crippetts
31 The Old Mill/The Temperance Hotel
32 Mill Cottage
33 Methodist Chapel/Leet Cottage
34 Bucks Cottage/Laburnum Cottage

8
7
1812

6½ 1906

1809

6
5
4

3 1830s

3½

2

1 c. 1830

Bucks Mills

34 1830s

The Car Park 1831?

15

Route Ways and Boundaries

It is important to try to understand how your place interacted with others in the vicinity. Relationships between settlements usually depend on the route ways that connect them. These change over time and the arrival, or departure, of a canal or railway can have a significant impact on links with other communities, as well as effecting the economy and migration patterns of your place. Historically, transport by water was easier than travelling overland, so rivers may well have been more important than roads, until well into the eighteenth century. What is now seen as the main road to the nearest market town, may not have been built until the 1800s. Modern changes, such as the construction of a by-pass, which will effect your community and its inhabitants, should also be recorded.

Maps are the obvious source for investigating route ways but do not neglect such things as directories,[7] which will list carriers' destinations. The title of Lt. Col. Daniel Paterson's book *A New and Accurate Description of all the Direct and Principal Cross Roads in England and Wales and Part of the Roads of Scotland,* indicates how useful this might be. It also contains references to some of the most important houses and their occupants. A facsimile of the 14th (1808) edition has been published (Lightening Source UK 2012).

The creation of turnpike trusts, canals and railways will have left a documentary trail. If the records of the companies themselves have been lost, there will still be mentions in newspapers or Parliamentary Papers.[8] An excellent site for details of English turnpike roads is **www.turnpikes.org.uk**.

When choosing your place you will have been aware of its boundaries. These are often prescribed by the limits of a parish or street. Occasionally, what constitutes a parish changes over time, so some One Place Studies will have to take this into account. It is interesting to see if there are natural features, such as rivers, that form the boundaries of your community. If your place is bounded by, or contains, hedges, you may be interested to know that natural historians estimate that a hedge gains an additional species of flora approximately every thirty years; so a hedge made up of five different shrubs or trees will be about 150 years old.

Project - Routeways

Use maps, directories and other relevant sources to suggest how people may have travelled to and from your place at different points in time. You might like to see how the arrival, or departure, of a new transport link effects such things as migration.[9]

Pictures[10]

Images of your place are important additions to your One Place Study. Providing you can visit your place, a series of up to date photographs of the local scenery, landmarks

---

[7] See Chapter 6, p. 33.
[8] See Chapter 6, p. 46.
[9] See Chapter 11, p. 75.
[10] See Chapter 5, p. 30, for ways to acquire images of people.

and buildings, both residential and non-residential, should be relatively easy to acquire. Historic photographs are even more valuable. You may be able to source some illustrations from Google Images via **www.google.co.uk** but remember that most of these will be copyright. The website MyHomesPast **www.myhomespast. co.uk/index.asp** invites people to submit photographs of homes over the years, in the hope of building up a longitudinal pictorial record of properties.

Other useful websites for obtaining photographs are:

Britain from Above **www.britainfromabove.org.uk** contains aerial views taken between 1919 and 1953.

Images of England **www.imagesofengland.org.uk** includes photographs and descriptions of English listed buildings.

PastScape **www.pastscape.org** provides details of nearly 400,000 records held in the National Historic Environment Database maintained by English Heritage. This mostly relates to listed properties and monuments and includes many pictures.

Francis Frith **www.francisfrith.com/uk** enables you to purchase historic images, old maps and books. There are also 'memory bank' entries for various places.

Heritage Images **www.heritage-images.com** also offer pictures for sale.

Old postcards are wonderful additions to your One Place Study. Postcard dealers will allow you to express an interest in a specific place but be mindful that this will probably have an impact on the price. You can also set up a 'saved search' on Ebay **www.ebay.co.uk**, so that you will receive notification if an item is listed relating to your place name. This is not the forum for a detailed explanation of copyright legislation but before storing or using images in any way, you should make sure that you are aware of the copyright implications.

Do not neglect images from the era before photography. Your place may have been sketched or painted. See the BBC's Your Paintings website **www.bbc.co.uk/arts/ yourpaintings** for an index of oil paintings.

Street, Farm and Field Names

The name of your place itself, as well as the names of the hamlets, streets, manors, farms and fields within it, are worth investigating. All may have implications for the origins of your place. For example, elements of the name may well suggest whether your place was Saxon, Norman or Norse in origin. The website of The English Place Name Society **www.nottingham.ac.uk/ins/placenamesociety/** includes a dictionary of words that make up English place names and a searchable guide to their interpretation. See also the Key to English Place-Names database **kepn. nottingham.ac.uk**. The Gazetteer of British Place Names **www.gazetteer.org.uk** gives only basic information but more detail can be purchased via the website. An excellent book on this subject is Mills, A D *A Dictionary of British Place Names* (Oxford University Press 2011). There are also many websites and books that analyse the place names of a region or county.

Project - Street, Farm and Field Name Survey

Identify the origin of the name of your place and note any spelling variations over time. Move on to the hamlet, street, manor, farm or field names in your community. Are they named for people, geographical features or events? What are the earliest instances of these names? Has the name been corrupted over the years? Some of the sources outlined in Chapter Nine will be very useful for identifying early place names within your community.

A Place Name Comparison

A thirteenth century tithe return lists properties in Buckland Brewer, Devon. Some are listed below with their modern equivalents where known.

Thornwiger	Thornwidger
Holewille	Holwell
Quercichene	
Oik	Oak
Sulclond	Silkland
Schorcterigge	Shortridge
Tudecote	Tithecott
Guvelandwrang	
Godekingeslond	Goutisland

Buildings

Most places will contain non-residential buildings, churches, shops, factories, mills, mines, railway stations and many more. These should all be included in your research. It is also important to look for dwellings that were formerly barns, chapels or had other non-domestic uses but have now been converted into houses. Consider the architectural styles of the buildings in your community. Given the difficulty and expense of transporting building materials, ordinary homes were constructed from what ever was handy. Thus vernacular architecture varies greatly across the land. Even the same form of construction may be known by another name in a different part of the country; Devonshire 'cob' is 'witchert' in Buckinghamshire.

Labourers' cottages were often built in similar styles for long periods, making dating difficult. See R W Brunskill's *Traditional Buildings of Britain: an introduction to vernacular architecture* (3rd revised edition Yale University Press 2006), *How to Read Houses: a crash course in domestic architecture* by Will Jones (The Bloomsbury Press 2013) and Trevor Yorke's *British Architectural Styles: an easy reference guide* (Countryside Books 2008). Useful websites are Looking at Buildings **www.lookingatbuildings.org.uk** and Bricks and Brass **www.bricksandbrass.co.uk**.

The best way to learn about the internal structure of the houses in your community is to download estate agents' details of properties, as they appear for sale on websites such as Zoopla **www.zoopla.co.uk** and Rightmove **www.rightmove.co.uk**.

Collecting a series of these over a period of years not only keeps you up to date with extensions and renovations but the changing prices make an interesting record. The details of older properties can be compared with their descriptions in the 1910 Inland Revenue Valuation Office Records.[11]

Look at the descriptions of the listed buildings in your community on Images of England **www.imagesofengland.org.uk**. Be aware that the dates quoted are based on architectural surveys and not on documentary evidence. As the same construction methods were common for many years, these dates can be inaccurate. See also the similar PastScape **www.pastscape.org**. In addition information about listed buildings can be found at **www.britishlistedbuildings.co.uk**.

The website **www.builderindex.org** allows searches in indexes to *The Builder* 1843-1852, *Building News* 1860-1920 and some other similar publications. These include descriptions and illustrations of a variety of domestic and public buildings. Searches can be made for place names, the name of the architect or the name or type of the building. The site contains links to downloads of some but not all, issues.

Specialist buildings, such as castles, mills, mines, limekilns and churches, may warrant particular research and require you to seek out relevant secondary literature and websites. Some suggestions have been included in the 'Further Reading' section of this chapter. The website Researching Historic Buildings in the British Isles **www.buildinghistory.org** is a good starting point.

Secondary Sources

Your place may have been the subject of articles and local history books, or be mentioned in books that cover a wider area. It is a good idea to seek out these secondary sources. For English communities, the Victoria County Histories are probably the first place to start. Unfortunately, some counties have not been well covered but their website **www.victoriacountyhistory.ac.uk** will show what has been produced. Not only can these scholarly volumes be useful in their own right but the footnotes may lead to many other books, articles and documents of relevance. The 'VCH Explore' section of their website gives access to a wide variety of interesting articles, illustrations and audio files. You are advised to search by place name, rather than by county, as in some cases, there appears to be nothing for a county, when in fact there is a great deal.

The journal *Notes and Queries* dates from 1849 and there are a number of county based versions, many of which are available online. These journals contain articles about history, literature and antiquarian matters. *Notes and Queries* is now published by Oxford University Press **nq.oxfordjournals.org/**. There are other antiquarian and historic journal that may also contain useful information. A county by county series of bibliographies, compiled by Stuart Raymond, lists many published works that could be relevant. See **www.stuartraymond.co.uk** for further details. The Bibliography of British and Irish History **www.royalhistoricalsociety.org/**

---

[11] See Chapter 6, p. 31.

respubs.php may also be helpful. This is an online subscription service listing hundreds of thousands of items, relating to British and Irish history.

Pevsner's county histories tend to concentrate on high status buildings but are worth consulting. See **www.pevsner.co.uk**. Publishers who specialise in local histories include Phillimore **www.phillimore.co.uk** and Halsgrove **www.halsgrove.com** and their catalogues may reveal publications covering your area. Your place may be the subject of a travelogue or journal. Vision of Britain **www.visionofbritain.org.uk** includes searchable transcripts of many historical travel writings, including the works of William Cobbett, Celia Fiennes and Daniel Defoe.

Many books or booklets relating to small localities have been written over the years; for example, guides to churches are common. These were often privately published and had very short print runs. Frequently, they have no ISBN and are therefore not held by the copyright libraries. There are three problems when trying to access such publications. Firstly, you need to be aware of their existence. Some may be listed on the appropriate parish page on Genuki **www.genuki.org.uk**. Others may appear in bibliographies, be located via an internet search or following an enquiry at the appropriate local library. Once you have discovered that a publication existed, the next problem is obtaining a copy. Local studies libraries, record offices and family history societies may be able to help. Internet searches, on sites such as **www.amazon.co.uk**, are another option. Finally, the quality of these publications varies tremendously. Some are well researched, interesting and accurate. Others are poorly written, based on guess work and contain flawed information.

Further Reading

Addison, Sir William *Understanding English Place-Names* (Batsford 1978).

Beech, G and Mitchell, R *Maps for Family and Local History* (National Archives 2004).

Brunskill, R W *Traditional Buildings of Britain: an introduction to vernacular architecture* (3rd revised edition Yale University Press 2006).

Field, J *English Field Names: a dictionary* (David and Charles 1972).

Gelling, Margaret *Signposts to the Past: place names and the history of England* (Phillimore 2010).

Gough, Richard and Hey, David (ed.) *The History of Myddle* (Penguin 1981).

Hewitt, Rachel *Map of a Nation: a biography of the ordnance survey* (Granta Books 2011).

Hindle, Paul *Maps for Historians* (Phillimore 1998).

Hindle, Paul *Medieval Roads and Tracks* (2nd ed. Shire Archaeology 2008).

Hollowell, Steven *Enclosure Records for Historians* (Phillimore 2000).

Hull, Lisa *Understanding the Castle Ruins of England and Wales: how to interpret the history and meaning of masonry and earthworks* (McFarland and co. 2009).

Jones, Edgar *Industrial Architecture in Britain 1750-1939* (Batsford 1985).

Jones, Will *How to Read Houses: a crash course in domestic architecture* (The Bloomsbury Press 2013).

Jowett, Alan *Jowett's Railway Atlas* (Guild Publishing 1989).

McNamara, Denis R *How to Read Churches: a crash course in ecclesiastical architecture* (Herbert Press Ltd. 2011).

Masters, Charles *Essential Maps for Family Historians* (Countryside Books 2009).

Mills, A D *A Dictionary of British Place Names* (Oxford University Press 2011).

The National Archives' Research Guide *Enclosure Awards*.

Oliver, George *Photographs and Local History* (Batsford 1989).

Oliver, Richard *Ordnance Survey Maps: a concise guide for historians* (2nd ed. Charles Close Society 2005).

Paterson, Lt. Col. David *A New and Accurate Description of all the Direct and Principal Cross Roads in England and Wales and Part of the Roads of Scotland* (Facsimile of the 14th (1808) edition Lightening Source UK 2012).

Rice, Matthew *Rice's Church Primer* (Bloomsbury Publishing 2013).

Pragnell, Hubert J *Industrial Britain: an architectural history* (Batsford 2000).

Smith, David *Maps and Plans for the Local Historian and Collector* (Batsford 1988). This volume is a guide to pre 1914 maps of the British Isles.

Winchester, Angus J L *Discovering Parish Boundaries* (Shire Publications 2000).

Wright, Geoffrey N *Turnpike Roads* (Shire Publications 2008).

Yarham, Robert *How to Read the Landscape* (A and C Black 2010).

Yorke, Trevor *British Architectural Styles: an easy reference guide* (Countryside Books 2008).

www.scotlandsplaces.gov.ukww
www.placenamesni.org

Chapter Three
Populating the Community

Population data

Your One Place Study should incorporate an investigation of population statistics. The online Historical Population Reports website **www.histpop.org** gives access to a complete collection of historical population reports from 1801 to 1937, covering Britain and Ireland. These include not only total populations but data such as the annual numbers of baptisms and marriages in a particular place. Vision of Britain **www.visionofbritain.org.uk** can also be searched by place and here you will find population figures and much more. The content varies from place to place but may include maps, a variety of statistics and descriptions of your place in historical writings. The Office for National Statistics is a useful site for recent statistics **www.ons.gov.uk/ons/index.html**; there is the option to browse by place or region. See in particular the webpages **www.neighbourhood.statistics.gov.uk**.

Scottish population figures can be found at **www.gro-scotland.gov.uk/census/index.html**. See also *Scottish Population Statistics including Webster's Analysis of Population 1755* (University of Edinburgh 1952) edited by James Gray Kyd, which can be downloaded from **www.gro-scotland.gov.uk/files2/the-census/Webster_final.pdf**.

Look for local population trends and see if they mirror what is going on in the rest of the county or country. Can you see the effects of urbanisation or rural depopulation? More recently, do the populations in rural areas reflect the vogue to 'escape to the country' at the end of the twentieth century?

Project - Population Analysis

Produce population pyramids for your area. To do this you need to know the age and gender of the residents of your place at a specific point in time. This is often only possible for the period for which census data is available. You may be able to compare your figures with national figures, or those for other areas.

For the period before census statistics are available, population analysis might consist of using the parish registers to record the numbers of baptism, marriages and burials in your place. Look for changes over time and trends such as peaks in burials, which may indicate an epidemic.

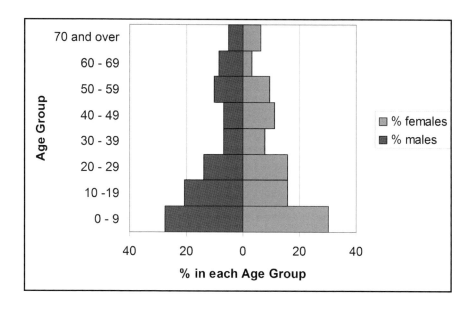

Project - Social Structure

Demographers have attempted to analyse and compare the social structure of communities using census returns or, to a lesser extent, other records that show occupation.[12] Occupations have to be allocated to a particular class. The most commonly used classifications are those devised by W A Armstrong.[13] These have been reprinted in Drake, Michael and Finnegan, Ruth *Sources and Methods for Family and Community History: a handbook* (Cambridge University Press 1994) and enable researchers to allocate most nineteenth century occupations to one of five social classes. These range from the professional people of Class One to the scavengers, labourers and charwomen of Class Five.

Analysing the social structure of your community is really only meaningful if you compare the findings at different times, or if you consider how your locality contrasts with others.

Collecting Biographical Information

People are an integral part of a One Place Study and whilst population figures might be interesting, your research only comes alive when you investigate the residents on an individual level. One way in which One Place Studies might be seen to differ from conventional local histories, is that they encompass the biographies of all the

---

[12] For example directories or post 1837 marriage registers.

[13] Armstrong, W A 'The Use of Information About Occupation' in Wrigley, E A (ed.) *Nineteenth-century Society: essays on the use of quantitative methods for the study of social data* (Cambridge University Press 1972) pp. 215-223.

inhabitants, not just the life stories of the more famous sons and daughters. Those with large One Place Studies may have to settle for collecting less detail about their inhabitants, or limiting their biographical research to just some of those who lived in their place. At least, most of those working on a One Place Study will maintain a database or card index of all those who have been found to live there.

The Oxford Dictionary of National Biography **www.oxforddnb.com** can be searched by place name. You need to log in via a subscribing institution, or using your local library card number.

Details of the lives of your inhabitants can be collected using almost all the sources described in the remainder of this book. This will add colour to the bald names and dates. It is also important to link these people together and this is explained further in Chapter Eleven.

Further Reading

Beresford, Maurice *The Lost Villages of England* (Sutton Publishing 1983).

Kyd, James Gray (ed.) *Scottish Population Statistics including Webster's Analysis of Population 1755* (University of Edinburgh 1952).

Wrigley, E A *Introduction to English Historical Demography* (Basic Books 1966).

Wrigley, E A; Davies, R S; Oeppen, J E and Schofield, R S *English Population History from Family Reconstitution 1580-1837* (Cambridge University Press 2005).

Wrigley, E A and Schofield R S *The Population History of England 1541-1871: a reconstruction* (Cambridge University Press 1989).

Part Two
Sources for One Place Studies

Chapter Four
Locating Sources

Much of the initial work of a One Place Study is the collection of data. Anything relating to your place should be seized upon with both hands. It may seem, at first, as if you are accumulating superfluous material but a less comprehensive approach risks missing vital information. Often it is the 'one-off' sources that relate only to your place, that are the most fascinating and informative. For example, there is a list of households who contributed to the restoration of the church bells at Parkham, Devon in 1874 that acts as an interim census. By their very nature, sources such as these cannot be included in this book. Do endeavour to locate them by studying any place indexes that may be available at local repositories, as well as following up the suggestions in this chapter.

When attempting to find relevant sources, the first port of call is likely to be the County Record Office that is local to your place of interest. It is however important to cast your net far more widely. For example, it is not surprising that there are records relating to Arreton, on the Isle of Wight, in the Isle of Wight Archives. As the Isle of Wight was once part of Hampshire, a researcher might reasonably look in Hampshire County Record Office and perhaps in Portsmouth Museum and Southampton City Archives. More surprisingly, records relating to this island parish have, so far, been found in the following locations:- West Sussex Record Office; The Corporation of London Record Office; The City of Westminster Archives; English Heritage National Monuments Records Office, Swindon; Lambeth Palace Library; Berkshire Record Office; The Museum of Rural Life, Reading; Wiltshire and Swindon Archives; Shakespeare Centre Archives, Stratford upon Avon and The East Riding of Yorkshire Archives. Indexes and catalogues, that help the One Place researcher to locate documents, are therefore invaluable.

You will also want to exhaust the resources of local studies libraries and The National Archives **www.nationalarchives.gov.uk**. Throughout this book mention is made of National Archives' Research Guides, these can be downloaded, free of charge via their website. Go to 'Records', 'Find Guidance' and then the appropriate letter of the alphabet.

The Access to Archives, or A2A, database now forms part of the website of The National Archives **www.nationalarchives.gov.uk/a2a/**. Searches are possible using keywords, so place names can be inserted in the search box. In this way, the

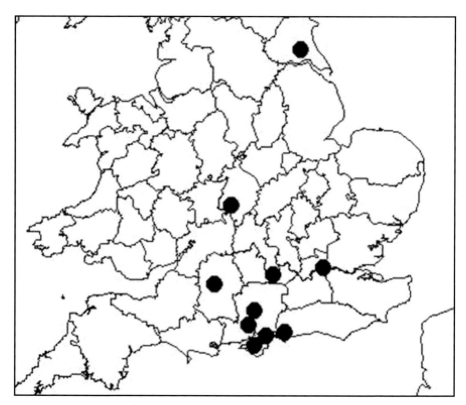

Location of Sources Relating to Arreton, Isle of Wight

catalogues of the many participating County Record Offices and other repositories, can be searched for documents relating to your place of interest. This is how many of those relating to Arreton, Isle of Wight were discovered. A2A is no longer being updated.

The National Archives are also responsible for The National Register of Archives. This enables researchers to locate estate archives, records of public and charitable bodies and similar private archives that are not in government repositories. The National Register of Archives can be searched free of charge at **www.nationalarchives. gov.uk/nra**. Scotland's free National Register of Archives is available at **www. nas.gov.uk/nras**. These Registers are indexes to collections only and not to individual documents. See also Archives Network Wales **www.archivesnet workwales.info/**.

The Archives Hub gateway website **archiveshub.ac.uk/** allows searches for archive collections held by over 200 institutions, primarily universities and colleges. To search the archives of more than a hundred institutions within Greater London, go to **www.aim25.ac.uk**. Here collection level descriptions include the records of

London livery companies, higher education institutions and learned societies. The records that are described may include material that relates to places outside London.

An umbrella site that enables a number of resources to be searched at once, either by place, personal name or keyword, is **www.connectedhistories.org**. Diverse documents for the period 1500-1900 that are included are: nineteenth century newspapers, a database of mid Victorian wood-engraved illustrations, Masonic records and a list of witches in early modern England.

British History Online **www.british-history.ac.uk** describes itself as a digital library containing some of the core printed primary and secondary sources for the medieval and modern history of the British Isles. Sources include: nineteenth century Ordnance Survey maps, journals of the House of Lords and House of Commons, the Survey of London, calendars of state papers, letters, diaries and a number of Gazetteers. A large number of regional documents are included and the site can be searched by surname or place name.

Local Record Societies may have transcribed and printed documents of relevance; these are particularly helpful for the period before 1600. The Royal Historical Society website **www.royalhistoricalsociety.org/textandcalendars.php** gives information about publications by Record Societies. Most Family History Societies publish data, either in book or digital form; these tend to be more recent sources. If at all possible, information gleaned from transcriptions should be verified with original documents.

If your place contains a property owned by English Heritage there may be relevant information concerning the whereabouts of sources on their Portico webpages **www.english-heritage.org.uk/professional/archives-and-collections/ portico/**.

Do not neglect three dimensional sources. If your place has been subjected to an archaeological survey, it may be of interest to read the resulting report. See The Council for British Archaeology **www.archaeology.co.uk**, which produces *Current Archaeology* Magazine. For links to other relevant websites go to **www.university archaeology.org.uk/for-students/clubs-societies.html**. It is also a good idea to contact your local county or district archaeological unit or society. Local finds, that are more than 300 years old, unearthed by amateur metal detectorists and members of the public, are listed on **http://finds.org.uk/**. The database on this site can be searched by place.

Chapters Five to Nine are arranged chronologically and describe a number of sources that might contribute to a One Place Study. The records mentioned relate primarily to England and Wales but many of the ideas and suggestions are applicable to those whose places are elsewhere. Some of these sources span several time periods but they have been included in the chapter relating to the era where they are most likely to begin to be useful. Many of these documents will be familiar to genealogists, family and local historians but it is likely that they will be used in a slightly different way by those conducting a One Place Study.

Chapter Five
After 1900

Oral Testimony and Memories

Each person who lives, or lived, in your community is a potential resource for your One Place Study. Their memories will give you access to information that is not found in official documents. The nature of oral evidence is such that you should make this a priority when beginning your One Place Study. Written sources will still be available when you are ready to use them, personal reminiscences may not.

Interviewing is a skill and before you begin, it is a good idea to read one of the books on oral history, listed in the 'Further Reading' section at the end of this chapter. The Oral History Society may also be useful, they have a website **www.oralhistory. org.uk** and produce a journal. The interviewer needs to remain inconspicuous and refrain from asking leading questions, or offering their own opinions. If you say 'the mill closed in 1965, didn't it?' and your subject is convinced it was 1966, they may be unwilling to disagree. Closed questions, those inviting a yes or no answer, are also not productive. 'Tell me what you did on a typical Sunday', will get a more useful response than 'Did you go to chapel?' Information is more likely to be forthcoming if the interviewer is known to and trusted by, the interviewee. Interviewing small groups at a time makes the subjects more relaxed and helps to spark memories but they may be reluctant to contradict each other.

Keep interviews reasonably short, certainly no more than an hour. Plan to revisit if necessary; this enables you to ask for clarification of comments made at the first interview. One Place interviews rarely require a structured, pre-planned series of questions. Have some broad topics in mind for each interview, such as the Blitz, farming, schooling, celebrations or the local factory. Be prepared to let the subject tell their own story, whilst keeping them from wandering completely off topic. If you have old photographs of your place, these can be a springboard for conversation. It is a good idea to ask your subjects in advance if they have a photographs of themselves or your place, which might contribute to your study.

There are no right or wrong ways to keep details of people's memories; all the possibilities have advantages and disadvantages. Recording, whether it be audio recording or videoing, can sometimes inhibit conversation. It requires equipment and the expertise to ensure that this works properly. The result will also need careful editing before it can be 'presented'. Writing notes is almost impossible if you are conducting the interview yourself. Even if you take a scribe who is fully proficient in shorthand, it is difficult to get a verbatim record. Which ever recording method you choose, it is usual to give the interviewee a copy, including any transcripts that you may make. Confidentiality and data protection are minefields and you should ensure that your interviewees are quite clear about how you intend using and publicising their contribution. Oral memories are copyright and you should have a permission form for your interviewees to sign, which sets out how their memories can be used.

It is important to try to track down former residents of your place, as their memories may contribute just as much as those who are still living in the area. They might be traced through advertisements or articles in the local paper or family history magazines. It may be possible to interview at a distance using Skype **www.skype. com**, Google+ **plus.google.com** or even the telephone. Written memories are also an option. As with the oral interviews, topic guidelines may be more appropriate than a structured questionnaire.

There may also be memories that were recorded in the past that are relevant. The problem here may be locating them. The British Sound Archive **cadensa.bl.uk/ uhtbin/cgisirsi/x/x/0/49/** or regional sound archives may be able to help. Written reminiscences, in the form of journals and letters are valuable additions to your One Place Study.[14] Some organisations, such as Women's Institutes, compiled books of memories to coincide with the millennium. Check the Francis Frith website **www.francisfrith.com/memories** for 'memory bank' entries for your place.

As part of the Mass Observation Survey, between 1937 and 1967 and again since 1981, ordinary people answered questions about everyday life in Britain, known as 'directive replies'. Others kept diaries that were submitted to the survey. The resulting archive is now housed at The Keep, as part of the University of Sussex's Special Collections **www.massobs.org.uk/index.htm**. The diaries and what are known as 'day surveys' from 1937-1938, can be searched by place but unfortunately the directive replies are only searchable by subject or personal name. The records themselves are not available online.

In 1986, to commemorate the 1000th anniversary of the Domesday Survey, many schools were involved in creating a snapshot of their community. This was made available online by the BBC in 2011, together with updates to the data. See Domesday Reloaded **www.bbc.co.uk/history/domesday** for details.

Project - Oral History

Conduct a series of oral history interviews. These might concentrate on a single aspect of your place's history or be more general. A good example of a specific oral history project is Dunkeswell's War Stories **dunkeswellwarstories.com.s161822. gridserver.com/**. Oral history can involve people of all ages, as interviewers and interviewees. You may wish to create a memory bank for the future by asking young people to record their impressions of living in your place in the twenty first century. Consider enlisting the help of media studies students from your local school, or encourage young people to make and post relevant YouTube videos **www. youtube.com**.

---

[14] See Chapter 2, Secondary Sources.

Photographs of People

Collecting photographs of the people who lived in your community will bring your One Place Study to life. The best way of going about this is to enlist the help of the residents themselves or their descendants. You should be able to get in touch with the latter through the family history network; see Chapter Three, 'Collecting Biographical Information'. Amassing a photographic archive gains momentum when you display any photographs you may have. This usually induces others to look out any they may have to add to your collection. If you can set up a mobile scanner during an exhibition or display, potential contributors will be reassured that they do not have to part with their precious photographs for scanning.

There are copyright and privacy issues. As with oral evidence, you are advised to get photograph owners to sign a form that gives you permission to use the photograph in specified ways. Be aware that if you publish photographs with living people in them you should attempt to get the consent of all those depicted, not just the owner of the picture. No pictures of those who are currently under the age of eighteen should be displayed or published without the written permission of their parents or carers.

Film and Television Archives

It may be that your place has been the subject of a film or television programme. The difficulty is being aware of this and then accessing the films. British Pathé **www.britishpathe.com** hold thousands of film clips that can be previewed online, their archive is searchable by place. The British Film Institute **www.bfi.org.uk/ archive-collections** hold an archive of film and television recordings that are searchable by keyword. There are also regional film archives such as The East Anglian Film Archive **www.eafa.org.uk** and The South West Film and Television Archive **www.plymouth.gov.uk/homepage/creativityandculture/archives/archive sswfta.htm**. Sadly much of this material is uncatalogued. See also The National Archives' **www.nationalarchives.gov.uk/education/focuson/film/film-archive** and Film Archives UK **filmarchives.org.uk**.

The Twentieth Century Censuses

The census returns are a key source for One Place Studies as they link people and places. For this reason, many One Place Studies begin with the indexing and analysis of census returns. This chapter considers the returns for 1901 and 1911; earlier censuses are covered in Chapter Six. You should aim to download images of the census returns for your place from one of the subscription or pay as you go websites such as Ancestry **www.ancestry.co.uk**, FindmyPast **www.findmypast.co.uk**, The Genealogist **www.thegenealogist.co.uk** or UK Census Online **www.uk censusonline.com**. Scottish censuses are also available via Scotland's People **www.scotlandspeople.gov.uk**. See also FreeCen **www.freecen.org.uk**, which gives free but incomplete, access to census transcripts. Ideally, you do not want to rely on transcripts made by others and should check these against the originals.

Censuses are arranged geographically. The 1901 census will reveal the residents of each household on census night, 31 March 1901. The address may not be as precise as you might wish. The number of rooms, if less than five, is recorded. For each individual, you will find name; gender; age; marital status; occupation; whether an employer, employee, self employed or working at home; place of birth and disability. The relationship of each person to the head of that household is also given, which helps with the reconstruction of family groups. Beware, this is the relationship to the *head* of the household only. The son of the head of the household is not necessarily also the son of his wife, whom the head may have married the previous day.

The 1911 census, taken on 2nd April, is in a slightly different format. After thirty years of compulsory education, it was thought that most households should be capable of filling in their own forms and one page is allocated to each family. The address is at the bottom right hand corner of the page and may only be a village name. Some of the subscription websites allow access to the enumerator's book lists of properties on their route. Occasionally these give more precise addresses. The number in the top right hand corner of the household form will help you to find the property on the enumerator's list. In this census, the number of rooms is given for all properties. There is also a question for married women about the number of years they have been married and the number of children, living and dead, of that marriage.

Project - Fertility and Infant Mortality

Use the 1911 census to conduct studies of fertility and infant mortality in your place. You could look at numbers of children born to each couple and the numbers who died. This is another study that may reveal contrasting results in different parts of your community.

The 1910 Inland Revenue Valuation Office Survey

This class of records is sometimes known as 'Lloyd George's Domesday'. In order to raise revenue, the Finance Act of 1909-1910 required a survey of all UK properties to be carried out. Site values of land on 9 April 1909 were recorded, with the intention being that, when properties changed hands, any increase in value, or capital gain, would be taxed at the rate of 20%. This related to the value of the site itself and not to any buildings or crops upon it. The act was repealed in 1920 and the First World War probably meant that fewer properties were changing hands but this is still a very useful One Place Study source for the period.

Ordnance Survey maps were used as a basis for giving every property a 'hereditament' number. These maps, held in Classes IR121 and IR124-135 in The National Archives, can be used to discover the hereditament number for a specific property. There is a facility via The National Archives' Research Guide *Valuation Office*,[15] which allows you to search for your place using a modern Ordnance Survey

---

[15] Available via their website **www.nationalarchives.gov.uk**.

map and thus obtain the full catalogue reference for the map that you need. Those conducting a One Place Study can probably omit this step, as it is likely that you will want to look at all the entries in one or more 'field book'. As a rough guide, most field books contain about 100 properties. The catalogue reference for the field book(s) for your place can be found using The National Archives' 'Discovery' catalogue advanced search facility. Search by putting in the place name AND IR58. These records recognise income tax parish names, which are not always what you might expect. Market Rasen, Lincolnshire, for example, is listed as East Rasen, not a place name that is generally recognised.

Landowners were required to give details of the land that they held, including a description, its value and the names of any tenants. Although the returns themselves rarely survive, the information, together with the details from the valuation books, was copied into the field books that now form Class IR58 at The National Archives. There are four pages allocated to every property or hereditament and the information from the landowners' returns is on the first page. This page may give details of when the tenancy commenced, how much rent was paid and who was responsible for repairs. Annotations may indicate any changes in tenant or owner during the lifetime of the legislation. The remainder of the entry includes a description of the property's construction, condition and number of rooms. Sometimes there is a sketch map, to show the position of outbuildings for example.

County Record Offices may hold draft copies of the maps and the original 'Form 37's. These were the provisional valuations, copies of which were sent to the land owners, together with other miscellaneous documentation relating to the act. Survival of these is very patchy but it is worth enquiring.

Project - Owner Occupiers

You can use the IR58 records to conduct a survey of the extent of owner occupation in your place. If you can identify each property on the ground, this might be depicted by colouring in the various properties on a map. Similarly, you could analyse the rents paid for particular properties. Comparisons could be made using the tithe schedules[16] or land tax returns[17] but remember that, in those documents, many sub-tenancies are not obvious.

Project - How Big is my House?

Use the IR58 records, together with census returns for 1891, 1901 and 1911, to assess the size of the properties in your place. All these documents give details of number of rooms that the property is deemed to have had.[18] You may be able to do this for the whole community or just a selected part. If you have collected modern estate agent's details[19] you could compare your findings with those. Again annotated maps may be the most appropriate way of presenting your findings.

---

[16] See Chapter 6, p. 42.   [17] See Chapter 7, p. 49.
[18] The 1891 and 1901 censuses only give the precise number of rooms if less than 5.
[19] See Chapter 2, Buildings p. 18.

Gazetteers and Directories[20]

Directories are very helpful for One Place Studies. They date from the mid eighteenth to the mid twentieth century, when they tended to be replaced by telephone directories and trade directories such as Yellow Pages. The earliest directories covered large towns and listed people of substance only. Rural areas are much less well served by directories. It is street directories, such as those produced by Kelly's, that will help you to find out who lived in each house. The gazetteer sections of directories give general descriptions of the area covering such things as acreage, terrain, population, trade, places of worship, schools, charities, gentry and their residences and transport links. Remember that there is a time lag between the collection of information and the publication of a directory. Thus a Directory of 1882 may well be recording addresses of residents a year or more earlier. An excellent book about the use of directories is Dennis R Mills' *Rural Community History from Trade Directories* (Local Population Studies 2001).

Runs of directories can be found in local studies and reference libraries or record offices. There are also good collections of directories in The Guildhall Library and the library of the Society of Genealogists. Historical Directories **www.historical directories.org** gives access to a wide range of digitised UK directories. The Gazetteer for Scotland website **www.scottish-places.info** is also very useful. There are several bibliographies of directories including Norton, Jane *Guide to National and Provincial Directories of England and Wales (excluding London) before 1856* (reprinted The Royal Historical Society 1984) and Shaw, Gareth and Tipper, Alison *British Directories: a bibliography and guide to directories published in England and Wales (1850-1950) and Scotland (1773-1950)* (Leicester University Press 1988). Kelly's, Pigot's and White's are the most widely available directories. There are also tourist guides, such as the Ward Lock Guides, which cover potential holiday areas. Not only do they describe the attractions of the area but the maps, photographs and advertisements are very useful sources of information about your place in the first half of the twentieth century. See **www.wardlockredguides.co.uk** for more information.

Electoral Registers

Electoral Registers list those who were entitled to vote and date from 1832, when the Reform Act extended the franchise, to the present day. Only about 20% of the male population were able to vote in 1832. Women do not appear until 1918 and were not granted the vote on the same basis as men until 1928. Early registers include details of the grounds upon which the individual was able to vote, such as by holding land or being a burgess or freeman. The registers are a good way of associating a person with a place but finding them is not straightforward. Some will be in record offices, more recent ones may still be with local authorities. Burgess lists of those entitled to vote,

---

[20] See Chapter 11, Services, Institutions and Societies, Project - Services and Chapter 11, Trades, Occupations and Industries, Project - Occupational Structure.

in borough elections run alongside Electoral Registers into the twentieth century but there are instances of surviving medieval Burgess Rolls. Gibson, Jeremy *Electoral Registers 1832-1948 and Burgess Rolls* (Family History Partnership 2008) is a useful county by county guide to the whereabouts of these records.

Council Minutes

District, Town and Parish Council minutes are useful sources for more recent information about your place. The difficulty is locating these documents. If they are not still held by the council, they may be in record offices and these should be your first port of call. The minutes will contain summaries of discussions about a variety of issues, such as planning applications, highways, allotments, the naming of roads, crime and grants. If councils own and rent out land, there may be information about this too.

War Memorials

The National Inventory of War Memorials project **www.ukniwm.org.uk** is being conducted under the auspices of the Imperial War Museum. It aims to record the location and other details of all war memorials in the United Kingdom, including the Channel Islands and the Isle of Man. These go far beyond village and town memorials to include those found in workplaces, schools, social clubs and elsewhere. It is important not to neglect these, often unseen, memorials. Currently, the database can be searched by location, important for One Place Studies but it will shortly be searchable by name as well.

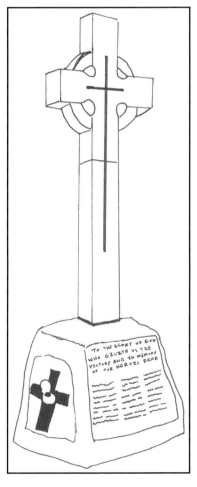

If you undertake any form of inventory of war memorials in your community you may wish to upload pictures to War Memorials Online **www.war memorialsonline.org.uk.** This site also allows people to express concerns about the condition of memorials.

Soldiers Died in the Great War

Soldiers Died in the Great War was published by the War Office in 1921, to record the officers and other ranks who were killed in action during the First World War. The eighty one volumes give details of 42,000 officers and 662,000 other ranks. The information usually consists of the soldiers' regiment, corps and battalion, decorations received, where the individual was born, lived and was enlisted, their rank and number and how, when and where they died. The books themselves are available in large libraries but they have also been digitised and made available with a searchable database on CD, by Naval and Military Press Limited **www.naval-military-press.com**. See also **www.great-war-casualties.com**. *Soldiers Died* is available online via Ancestry UK **www.ancestry.co.uk** or FindmyPast **www.findmypast.co.uk**. Unfortunately, these options allow searches by name but not by place, so you will need to have discovered the list of individuals for your community from another source, such as the war memorial.

Commonwealth War Graves Commission

The website of the Commonwealth War Graves Commission **www.cwgc.org** contains records of 1,700,000 members of the Commonwealth forces who lost their lives and civilians who died as a result of enemy action, during the two world wars. Technically there is no place search facility but using the advanced search, your place can successfully be entered in the additional information box and nothing further is required. The resulting information will include:- name, rank, service number, date of death, age, regiment or service, country for whom served, grave reference and cemetery or memorial. There may also be further details such as place of birth, address and next of kin.

Rolls of Honour

Rolls of Honour list casualties of war, some include those who served but survived. Two useful websites are **www.roll-of-honour.org.uk** and **www.roll-of-honour.com**. A number of rolls are available on Ancestry **www.ancestry.co.uk** and FindmyPast **www.findmypast.co.uk**. Most online rolls are searchable by name not place, so can only be used for One Place Studies in conjunction with other records.

The National Roll of Honour for the First World War (reprinted Naval and Military Press 2007) consists of fourteen volumes, each based on a different geographical area. The coverage is not complete, for example Wales and the South West are not included but it does contain 100,000 short biographies. It is available in large reference libraries and via FindmyPast **www.findmypast.co.uk**. The information differs from other similar sources, such as *Soldiers Died in the Great War*, because it came from the families of those who served and not from the official records.

The five volumes of *De Ruvigny's Roll of Honour 1914-1918* (reprinted Naval and Military Press 2003) contain biographies of over 26,000 casualties, both officers and other ranks, of the First World War. The biographies of personnel from all branches of military service were compiled between 1914 and 1924, with the majority of the entries being from the beginning of this period. The amount of information, varies from name, regiment or ship, place and date of death to more detailed biographies including photographs. This roll is searchable by name on Ancestry **www. ancestry. co.uk** and FindmyPast **www.findmypast.co.uk**.

There are also regional, regimental, school, company and association rolls of honour. These may be more difficult to track down but the centenary of the outbreak of the First World War has meant that many researchers are concentrating on this period so more are becoming accessible online. For example, the Friends of Devon Archives **www.foda.org.uk** are transcribing the county Roll of Honour, to make it available to researchers. The Welsh Centre for International Affairs are digitising the Welsh Roll **www.wcia.org.uk**.

The Army Roll of Honour for the Second World War is held at The National Archives in Class WO304. It can be searched by name on FindmyPast **www. findmypast.co.uk**.

Absent Voters' Lists

In the run up to the 1918 general election, procedures were put into place to allow servicemen who were not at home to be able to vote. The Absent Voters' Lists, which are in County Record Offices, record names, home addresses, ship, regiment, service number and rank. For details of online access to some lists see **www.1914-1918.net** then 'How to Research a Soldier' and 'Insights and Articles'. Research often focuses on those who perished in conflicts. This source enables those who served and survived to be recorded as well.

Project - World War One

Use your local war memorial(s), the Commonwealth War Graves Commission database, rolls of honour and *Soldiers Died in the Great War* to compile a list of those from your community who lost their lives in this conflict. Add as much biographical information as you can. Local newspapers, particularly the issue shortly after the death of a serviceman, can be very useful but remember that some deaths were not reported until long afterwards. Memoirs and photographic evidence may enhance your research. If you do not have a photograph of the serviceman himself, you could take pictures of his former home, his gravestone or his entry on a Commonwealth War Graves Commission memorial. You could also find each soldier in the 1911 census and in local school records or look for his home in the Valuation Office Records. If you wish to take this research further you could seek additional details from regimental diaries and other service records. For those who perished, there may be a soldier's will that could be downloaded from **probatesearch.service.gov.uk**. You can look at maps of the trenches where the soldiers may have served at **http://repository. mcmaster.ca/fedora/repository/macrepo%3A49/-/collection**. The subscription website Forces War Records **www.forces-war-records.co.uk** may be helpful.

See **www.bbc.co.uk/history/ww2peopleswar/**

This type of project may well be one in which you could involve school aged children, with each small group of children taking one or two names from the local war memorial for example.

Do not ignore those who served and survived. Absent Voters' Lists are the best source for this. It may be possible to obtain further information from Classes WO363 and WO364 at The National Archives. These contain service and pension records for non commissioned officers and other ranks serving between 1914 and 1920. The records are available for a fee via Ancestry **www.ancestry.co.uk**, yet again these can only be searched by name. Similarly, those who were invalided out of the services and awarded the Silver War Badge, can be search by name on Ancestry. There are also prisoner of war records at The National Archives. See their Research Guide *Looking for Records of a British Prisoner of War c.1790-1919* downloadable from **www.nationalarchives.gov.uk** for further information. Once you are aiming for this level of detail, you will need to consult specialist guides to military research, several of which have been included in the 'Further Reading' for this chapter.

Although some of the suggested sources for the First World War are not applicable, you can also research the service personnel of the Second World War. For this conflict, you are more likely to be able to find oral evidence from the children of those who served if not from the individuals themselves.

Your Community at War

The Imperial War Museum's Lives of the First World War project **www.livesofthe firstworldwar.org/** is a huge archive of material relating to this conflict and you may wish to contribute memories or photographs relating to your place. Whilst

thinking about communities at war, it is worth mentioning the website Bomb Sight **www.bomb sight.org**, which records bomb damage during the London Blitz. If your place is outside London, there are a few sites which cover some other areas, such as The Hull Blitz **www.rhaywood.karoo.net/ bombmap.htm**. It is also worth enquiring if your local record office or local studies library has similar maps for your area. There may also be maps of air raid precautions; **www.cyber-heritage.co.uk/ history/sector. htm** shows those for Plymouth.

If your place is rural, it is likely to have been the recipient of evacuees during the Second World War. This too can be a topic for study although it is difficult to find information. School records and newspapers might be a good place to start. Some areas had evacuees' associations but these are now winding down as there are fewer surviving evacuees. There may be surviving records in local record repositories.

Land Registry

The Land Registry website **www.landregistry.gov.uk** allows you to purchase copies of title registers, giving recent ownership details and title plans showing the extent of the property. This is only available for properties that have changed hands since the legislation was introduced in 2000. The information is fairly minimal, so this may only be something that you resort to on rare occasions. Beware of commercial sites that mimic the official land registry site and will charge you much more for the same information.

National Farm Survey

During the Second World War, the Ministry of Agriculture had to ensure that all holdings of three acres or more were being sufficiently efficient and productive. The need to monitor agricultural productivity meant that parish lists, compiled in June 1940, of farmers and their addresses survive in Class MAF65 at The National Archives. These are arranged by county and then parish. Surveys were carried out between 1941 and 1943, leading to the creation of a series of documents for each farm that are now in Class MAF32. The records are arranged by parish and the three sets of forms that resulted are bundled separately. There is also a collection of maps in Class MAF73, which show the farms that were included.

The first form, B496/E.1, gives the address, the Ordnance Survey map reference, the owner, the occupier, the form of tenure and details of whether the farmer was full or part time. It also gives the farmer's other occupation if applicable. In addition, it records details of any other landholdings, the situation, access, type of soil, land use and the number of cottages associated with farm. The condition of the buildings, fences, drains and ditches are also described. Form C51/554 lists the crops grown and C47.5.5.4 gives information about labourers, automotive power, rent and length of occupancy. Sadly, some of these forms were sparingly completed.

The National Archives also hold parish level statistics relating to the numbers of farmers and farms, the acreages of crops and pasture and the number of livestock. These are in Class MAF68. They date from 1866 but were not compulsory until 1917.

Project - Farms and Farming

The National Farm Survey can be used as a basis for researching farming practices in your area. You can study the extent of owner occupation and this can be compared with the Valuation Office information or with that in the tithe schedules[21] or land tax returns.[22] The National Farm Survey can also be used to look at how many farmers also had other occupations. If you use these records to study land use in your place, your findings could again be compared with the information from the tithe schedule.[23]

---

[21] See Chapter 6, p. 42.   [22] See Chapter 7, p. 49.   [23] See Chapter 6, p. 42.

Further Reading

Atkins, P J *The Directories of London 1677-1977* (Marcell 1980).

Beckett, Ian *The Home Front 1914-1918: how Britain survived the Great War* (The National Archives 2006).

Beech, Geraldine and Mitchell, Rose *Maps for Family and Local History: records of the tithe, valuation office and National Farm Survey of England and Wales 1836-1943* (2nd ed. National Archives 2004).

Calder, Angus *The People's War: Britain 1939-1945* (Jonathan Cape 1969).

Caunce, Stephen *Oral History for Local Historians* (Longman 1994).

Chapman, Philip J *Basic Approach to Illuminating your Family History with Picture Postcards* (Federation of Family History Societies 2000).

Christian, Peter and Annal, David *Census: the expert guide* (The National Archives 2008).

Fowler, Simon *Tracing Your Army Ancestors: a guide for family historians* (2nd ed. Pen and Sword 2013).

Fowler, Simon *Tracing your Naval Ancestors: a guide for family historians* (Pen and Sword 2011).

Ginn, Peter, Goodman, Ruth and Langlands, Alex *Wartime Farm: rediscovering the skills and spirit of World War II* (Pavilion Books 2012).

Hart, Cynthia *Tell me your Story: how to collect and preserve your family's oral history* (Workman Publishing 2009).

Hodge, Susie *The Home Front in World War Two: keep calm and carry on* (Remember When 2013).

Holding, Norman *World War I Army Ancestry* (revised and updated by Iain Swinnerton 4th ed. Society of Genealogists 2004).

Howarth, Ken *An Oral History Handbook* (Sutton 1999).

Ingham, Mary *Tracing your Servicewoman Ancestors* (Pen and Sword 2012).

Jolly, Emma *Tracing your Ancestors using the Census* (Pen and Sword 2013).

Lord, Evelyn *Investigating the Twentieth Century: sources for local historians* (Tempus Publishing 2004).

McLaughlin, Eve *Twentieth Century Research* (Varney's Press 2000).

Mills, Dennis R *Rural Community History from Trade Directories* (Local Population Studies 2001).

The National Archives' Research Guide *National Farm Surveys of England and Wales 1940-1943.*

The National Archives' Research Guide *Valuation Office Survey.*

Norton, Jane *Guide to National and Provincial Directories of England and Wales (excluding London) before 1856* (reprinted The Royal Historical Society 1984).

Pappalardo, Bruno *Tracing your Naval Ancestors* (The National Archives 2003).

Perks, Robert *The Oral History Reader* (2nd edition Routledge 2006).

Pols, Robert *Dating Nineteenth Century Photographs* (Federation of Family History Societies 2005).

Pols, Robert *Dating Twentieth Century Photographs* (Federation of Family History Societies 2005).

Pols, Robert *Family Photographs 1860-1945* (PRO 2002).

Raymond, Stuart A *The Census 1801-1911: a guide for the internet era* (Family History Partnership 2009).

Raymond, Stuart A *Tracing your Twentieth Century Family History* (Federation of Family History Societies 2003).

Raymond, Stuart *The Home Front 1939-1945: a guide for family historians* (Family History Partnership 2012).

Ritchie, Donald A *Doing Oral History* (2nd edition OUP USA 2005).

Shaw, Gareth and Tipper, Alison *British Directories: a bibliography and guide to directories published in England and Wales (1850-1950) and Scotland (1773-1950)* (Leicester University Press 1988).

Shrimpton, Jayne *Family Photographs and How to Date Them* (Countryside Books 2008).

Shrimpton, Jayne *How to get the most from Family Pictures* (Society of Genealogists 2011).

The Society of Genealogists *Catalogue of Directories and Poll Books in the Possession of the Society of Genealogists* (Society of Genealogists 1994).

Spencer, William *Army Records: a guide for family historians* (The National Archives 2008).

Spencer, William *First World War Army Service Records: a guide for family historians* (The National Archives 2008).

Tate, W E *The English Village Community and the Enclosure Movements* (Gollancz 1967).

Tomaselli, Philip *The Second World War 1939-1945: military history sources for family historians* (Federation of Family History Societies 2006).

Watts, Michael J and Christopher T *My Ancestor was in the British Army: a guide to British army sources for family historians* (2nd ed. Society of Genealogists 2009).

Chapter Six
The Nineteenth Century

The Nineteenth Century Censuses
You may well have already collected and analysed data from the twentieth century census returns. It is important to extend this back into the nineteenth century. Most of the comments concerning access to and the use of these records, made in Chapter Five, also apply to earlier census returns. The mid nineteenth century censuses do not contain quite as much information as those of the twentieth century; the 1841 census is noticeably less informative. Do check to see if your place is one of the handful for which returns of 1801-1831 survive. See Gibson, Jeremy and Medlycott, Mervyn *Local Census Listings 1522-1930: holdings in the British Isles* (Federation of Family History Societies 1997) for details of what is available.

If your place is a hamlet or street, you may have difficulty in identifying it within a parish, as the census address frequently will just read 'village'. Farm names to tend to be included but often the labourers' cottages on the farm appear with the same address. It is important to use the census returns, in conjunction with other documents such as the Land Tax[24] and Tithe Records, to try to associate the census households with a specific property.

Project - Household Structure
Use the census returns for your place to examine the composition of the households within it. A simple analysis of the numbers of people in each house is a good start. You can build on this to consider how many households are single occupancy and how many contain couples, nuclear families or three generational groups. Look at the incidence of live-in servants, boarders and lodgers.[25] Do these patterns vary in different parts of your place, or over time? You might do this on the basis of either houses or households. Multi-occupancy was common, with separate households sharing a single dwelling. Houses should be indicated in the returns, as should new households within that dwelling. This is done slightly differently in different returns, for example by single and double marginal lines in 1841 and underlining in 1851. It does not matter whether you base your research on a house or a household but you do need to be consistent.

Project - Disability in Your Place
The disability columns of the census returns can be used to study the incidence of disability in your place. Be aware that the not very politically correct descriptors had

---

[24] See Chapter 7, p. 49.
[25] Technically, a boarder was provided with food, whereas a lodger was not but the distinctions do blur.

no precise definition and the 'diagnosis' will have been made by an untrained enumerator. Notwithstanding this, you can record the numbers of individuals stated to have a particular disability and see if this changes over time.

Tithe Schedules

The Tithe Maps have already been mentioned in Chapter Two 'Maps'. The accompanying schedules allow you to identify the owners, occupiers, area, land use and value of each numbered plot on the map. The schedules are housed with the maps. The National Archives' copies are in Class IR29. The tithe records can be very helpful when trying to associate 1841 census entries with specific buildings. One drawback is that sub tenancies may not be apparent. In addition, some rows of cottages were grouped together in one plot number and the occupiers may be listed as, for example, 'Robert Clarke and others'.

Project - Land Use

Use the tithe records to research land use in your place. You might colour a copy of the tithe map to indicate, arable land, orchards, rough grazing or pasture.

Ecclesiastical Census

To accompany the 1851 census, a series of questions were sent to the leaders of all congregations, of whatever denomination. The returns describe, for each place of worship, the location, date of erection or foundation, the name of the minister and the size of the congregation on 30th March 1851. The originals are at The National Archives in Class HO129, arranged by county and Poor Law Union. The returns have been published for some counties. They are important records for forming an impression of the religious complexion of your place in the mid nineteenth century.

Non-conformist Records

Not all the residents of your place will have been members of the Anglican Church and it is important to seek out records of any other denomination that had a presence in your place. You may need to consult books that help with research into the specific denominations that you encounter; some are included in the further reading for this chapter. There may be records of baptisms, marriages and burials, minute books of the governing bodies of the place of worship and other useful material. These may be with the congregations, in County Record Offices or held centrally. There are a wide variety of records that you may be able to utilise. For example, inhabitants of your place may be among the million Wesleyan Methodists who contributed to the 'Million Guinea Fund', also known as the 'Twentieth Century Fund'. The resulting Historic Roll is held at Methodist Central Hall in London and they will answer enquiries. The rolls give names and addresses of contributors who donated their guineas between 1899 and 1904.

Project - Worship in Your Place

Build up a picture of faith in your place by seeking information about the religious buildings and the worshippers. The Ecclesiastical Census is a good starting point but many churches and chapels were founded in the second half of the nineteenth century. Newspapers can be helpful and may report the opening or closure of places of worship or give details of their renovation. Remember that many chapels were used by different denominations during their history and may now be private dwellings. Bring the study up to date by including mosques, temples and multi-faith centres that may have been established in your place more recently. You might also look at the biographies of the clergymen, elders, ministers and other religious leaders who have held office in your place.

Cemetery and Crematoria Records

As churchyards became full, increasing numbers of those who lived in your place will have been buried in cemeteries or will have been cremated. Cemeteries and crematoria will often cover a much wider area than just your place. It may be possible to locate relevant burials or cremations. How difficult this is will depend on how well the records have been indexed. In addition, there needs to be the ability to use the abode of the deceased as a search term. The records may be with the local authority or held at the cemetery itself. Some cemeteries have groups of friends who have worked to provide online access to their interments.

School Records

Schools are an important institution in your place. Many schools were opened in the early years of the nineteenth century, either under the auspices of The British and Foreign Schools Society **www.bfss.org.uk**, which was founded by Quaker Joseph Lancaster in 1808 or the The National Society (formerly The National Society for Promoting the Education of the Poor in the Principles of the Established Church) **www.churchofengland.org/education/national-society.aspx**, which was formed three years later. The former were intended to be non-denominational so were favoured by the non-conformists, whilst the latter was an Anglican foundation. The archives of the British and Foreign School Society are at Old School House, 1 Hillingdon Hill, Uxbridge, Middlesex UB10 0AA. Records include minute books, accounts, correspondence and inspection reports. The National Society records are at The Church of England Record Centre, 15 Galleywall Rd, London SE16 3PB. There may be earlier private schools for the better off that you might become aware of through Ecclesiastical Visitations.[26]

Once Board Schools were introduced, between 1870 and 1880, the number of records increase. These include Admissions Registers, which give the date of entry of each pupil, their date of birth, address and the names of their parents or guardians.

---

[26] See Chapter 7, p. 50.

There is also information about any previous school and the destination of those who leave. The address column is particularly useful, as these may be more precise than addresses given in the census returns. For information about Scottish Admissions Registers see **www.scan.org.uk/knowledgebase/topics/schooladmissions. htm**. You may also be able to find Log Books, which date from 1862, Punishment Books and Minutes of School Boards or Governors. The local County Record Office should be your first place of enquiry but some records remain with the schools. There is a recent tendency for schools to 'federate'; whilst remaining separate entities, they share a head and governing body. This might precipitate the removal of records to the wrong school, or lead to their disposal. A similar problem occurred when the comprehensive system was introduced after 1965.

Teachers' Registration Council Registers from 1914-1948 are available on FindmyPast **www.findmypast.co.uk**. As some of the 1914 registrants had been teaching for many years, they contain details of more than 100,000 English and Welsh teachers who were working between 1870 and 1948. Not all teachers joined the register. The cards give name, date of registration, address, 'attainments', training and a list of schools where they worked, together with the dates. Unfortunately these are not searchable by place but they can be used once the names of the teachers have been obtained from other sources. The originals are at The Society of Genealogists.

The National Archives hold some records of relevance, such as Class ED2, which contains parish files, plans of extensions to buildings and inspectors' reports and recommendations. Inspectors' reports can also be found in Classes ED51, ED53 and ED196. There are several National Archives' Research Guides relating to schools and education.

Project - Education in Your Place

Use sources such as school records, census returns, directories,[27] ecclesiastical visitations[28] and newspapers to build up a picture of education in your place. Newspaper archives can be searched for 'place name AND school', which should give many hits. Check whether the school compiled a centenary booklet or has other details of its own history. Research the biographies of the teachers in your place. Remember that a number of the schoolmistresses in the mid nineteenth century census returns would have been in charge of dame schools and may have been little more than baby minders. It is also possible for a teacher to live in your place and not work there. When you begin the hunt for photographs of residents of your place, it is often school photos that come out of the woodwork first; sadly often lacking names. These usually create a great deal of interest at exhibitions or displays. These sources, taken together with oral evidence, should make it possible to form a reasonable impression of schooling and school teachers in your community.

---

[27] See Chapter 5, p. 33.
[28] See Chapter 7, p. 50.

Rent and Rate Books

Particularly if your place is in a more urban area, there may be rate books that you can access at your local record office. From the nineteenth century, rates were collected for such things as the maintenance of highways or the provision of sanitation in boroughs and towns. Some earlier rate books do survive but these are rare. If parts of your place were owned by an estate there may be similar rent books, that will link occupants with a particular property. The latter may be in private archives, so are less easy to access. It is worth the effort however especially if you can locate a run of rent or rate books covering a span of years.

Newspapers

Newspapers are a very rich source of information for your One Place Study. Fortunately the British Newspaper Library has made digital images of many national and local papers available online at **www.britishnewspaperarchive.co.uk**. This material is also available via FindmyPast **www.findmypast.co.uk**. Searching is free but the downloading of images requires a subscription. Both options allow you to search by place name. You can add a theme, such as 'Grimsby AND fishing', if you are concentrating on a specific piece of research. Unfortunately, the poor quality of some early newspapers means that the optical character recognition, which has been used to create the index, may lead to results that are scrambled sufficiently for entries to be missed.

Be aware that there may be locally held papers that do not form part of the British Newspaper archive collection. Local Record Offices may have complete runs of a particular title, whereas those that have been digitised might have gaps. There may also be useful indexes to newspapers in local repositories.

In addition, you may wish to search The Times Digital Archive **gale. cengage.co.uk/times.aspx/**, which is often available free through your public library and the Burney collection of seventeenth and eighteenth century newspapers at **gdc.gale.com/products/17th-and-18th-century-burney-collection-newspapers/**. Links to further online newspaper sources can be found in The National Archives' Research Guide *Newspapers*. The National Library of Wales is digitising approximately a million pages of Welsh newspapers and journals. See **www.llgc.org.uk/index.php?id=4723** for details.

To find out which publications covered your area, consult Gibson, Jeremy *Local Newspapers 1750-1920, England and Wales; Channel Islands; Isle of Man: a select location list* (3rd ed. Family History Partnership 2011). For details of current local newspapers see the annually issued *Willing's Press Guide*.

The London Gazette, published from 1665 and its Scottish and Irish equivalents are now all searchable and downloadable at **www.thegazette.co.uk**. The information will include details of promotions of service personnel, clerics and members of the legal profession, lists of bankrupts and prisoners, notice of the formation or dissolution of partnerships and companies and much more.

Project - Your Place in the News

Using online and other indexes, collect references to your place in historic and modern newspapers. Even quite small places are likely to be mentioned frequently, so you may well amass a sizeable archive. Whether you are storing digital or paper images, you are advised to create some kind of index of personal names, house names and themes, to help you locate relevant entries.

Parish Magazines

Clergy began using parish magazines to keep in touch with their parishioners in the mid nineteenth century. These gradually became more popular and more economically viable as the century progressed. The sort of information that you may find in these magazines is: details of services; baptisms, marriages and burials; obituaries of prominent church goers; names of clergy and churchwardens; social events; donations to the church; prizes awarded to Sunday scholars and Sunday School treats.

The non-conformist equivalents, such as Methodist Circuit Magazines, are equally informative. The main difficulty is accessing these magazines as, particularly in rural parishes, the print runs may have been small and survival patchy to non-existent. There may be some in local studies libraries or archives or even with the church itself. You are most likely to come across isolated copies in private hands that have perhaps been kept because they record a family baptism or marriage.

Many congregations still issue monthly newsletters and a collection of these could form part of your One Place Study.

Union Workhouse Records

If your place is a town, it may have had a Union Workhouse, established under the Poor Law Amendment Act of 1834. The inmates would have included people from the surrounding villages as well as residents of your town. As an institution within your community, an investigation of the history of the workhouse should form part of a One Place Study. There may be records such as minutes of the meetings of the Board of Guardians, admissions registers, burial registers and correspondence available in the County Record Office. Chapter 11, 'Services, Institutions and Societies' contains more information about workhouses.

Parliamentary Papers

Parliamentary Papers included reports, accounts and surveys ordered by Parliament, including the results of enquiries by select committees and royal commissions. You may also find your place referred to in private members' bills or 'local and personal acts', encompassing such matters as enclosure, railways, canals, bridges and the installing of drainage or gas. These bills come under the category of sessional papers or 'blue books'. The easiest method of access is via **parlipapers.chadwyck.co.uk** but you need to do this via a registered institution, such as a university or library. The website gives further background information. See also Powell, W R *Local History from Blue Books* (Historical Association 1962). Once you have downloaded a pdf copy of a particular report, the text of the papers is fully searchable but there is no composite index to the contents. You will need to look at the titles of the many thousand papers to see if it seems likely that your place may get a mention. There is a wealth of information in these papers, including witness statements from named individuals about such things as living and working conditions. Stephens, W B *Sources for English Local History* (revised edition Cambridge University Press 1981) contains a large section about these records and anyone planning on using them might like to read his guidance.

Further Reading

Berry, George *Discovering Schools* (Shire Publications 1970).

Bourne FW *The Bible Christians: their origins and history* (reprinted Tentmaker Publications 2004).

Breed, G R *My Ancestors were Baptists* (Society of Genealogists 1986).

Chapman, Colin R *The Growth of British Education and its Records* (Lochin 1991).

Christian, Peter and Annal, David *Census: the expert guide* (The National Archives 2008).

Gibson, Jeremy and Medlycott, Mervyn *Local Census Listings 1522-1930: holdings in the British Isles* (Federation of Family History Societies 1997).

Gibson, Jeremy *Local Newspapers 1750-1920, England and Wales; Channel Islands; Isle of Man: a select location list* (3rd ed. Family History Partnership 2011).

Higginbotham, Peter *The Workhouse Encyclopaedia* (The History Press 2012).

Jolly, Emma *Tracing your Ancestors using the Census* (Pen and Sword 2013).

Joseph, Dr Anthony *My Ancestors were Jewish* (4th ed. Society of Genealogists 2008).

Leary, William *My Ancestors Were Methodists: how can I find out more about them?* (Society of Genealogists 4th edition 2005).

Milligan, Edward H and Thomas, Malcolm J, *My Ancestors were Quakers* (2nd edition Society of Genealogists 1999).

The National Archives' Research Guide *Census*.

The National Archives' Research Guide *Census: further research*.

The National Archives' Research Guide *Newspapers*.

Powell, W R *Local History from Blue Books* (Historical Association 1962).

Raymond, Stuart A *The Census 1801-1911: a guide for the internet era* (Family History Partnership 2009).

Ratcliffe, Richard *An Introduction to Methodist Records* (Family History Partnership 2014).

Ratcliffe, Richard *Basic Facts about the Wesleyan Methodist Historic Roll* (Federation of Family History Societies 2005).

Stephens, W B and Unwin, R W *Materials for the Local and Regional Study of Schooling 1700-1900* (British Records Association 1987).

Wenserul, Rosemary *Tracing Your Jewish Ancestors: a guide for family historians* (Pen and Sword 2008).

Chapter Seven

The Eighteenth Century

Manorial Records

Manorial Court Rolls can be an informative addition to the resources of your One Place Study and might date back to the period before parish registers. The first problem is to identify which manor, or manors, had jurisdiction in your place. There may have been several manors in a parish or a manor might spread across more than one parish, perhaps with detached portions some distance away. Once the relevant manors have been ascertained, you then need to find out where any surviving records might be. Manorial records do not survive well but are often in County Record Offices or in private hands. The Manorial Documents Register, which helps with the identification of manors and the locating of their records, is now held by The National Archives. The webpage **www.nationalarchives.gov.uk/mdr** gives access to the Manorial Documents Register for many counties and others will follow. For those counties not yet available online, there is a microfilm copy at The National Archives. Three National Archives' research guides are relevant: *Manors*; *Manors: further research* and *Using the Manorial Documents Register and how to find Manorial Lordships*.

The problems with using manorial records do not stop there. They are in Latin until 1733 and many abbreviations were used. It is well worth persevering however as they are full of fascinating information. To begin with, there are lists of the transfer of copyhold land, often with accounts of previous holders going back several generations. This is vital for linking individuals to your place, as well as helping to reconstruct the genealogies of the landholders. The court rolls also contain lists of attendees at the manorial court. Accounts of minor misdemeanours, relating to such things as public nuisance, slander and affray, help to bring the people of your place to life.

Land Tax Returns

Land Taxes were raised from the late seventeenth century until the 1950s. Their use, for the purposes of One Place Studies, is likely to be for the period 1780-1832. The records were particularly well kept at this time, as the lists were used to identify those entitled to vote. The annual returns record taxable land, normally holdings of an acre or more, with the name of the property, the owner, the occupier and value. Most returns are to be found in County Record Offices, filed with the Quarter Sessions records. There are copies of the 1798 returns for England and Wales[29] in Class IR23

---

[29] With the exception of Flintshire.

at The National Archives. From 1798, it was possible to 'commute' the tax by paying fifteen times the annual rate, in order to be exonerated from any future liability. This means that, from this date, the returns become less complete. For a county by county list of the whereabouts of surviving records see Gibson, Jeremy; Medlycott, Mervyn and Mills, Dennis *Land and Window Tax Assessments* (2nd edition Federation of Family History Societies 1998). The only Scottish Land Tax records to survive are those for Midlothian 1799-1812. Similar information for Scotland can be found in the Registers of Sasines and from 1855, in annual Valuation Rolls.

If your place has a reasonably good run of surviving Land Tax Returns, they can be combined with the tithe schedules and the 1841 census to take your record of properties and their occupiers back from the mid nineteenth century into the eighteenth century.

Parish Chest

Parish chest records, if they survive, should be consulted as part of your One Place Study. Apart from the parish registers themselves, which are discussed in Chapter 9, these varied documents might include churchwardens' accounts, which list the more affluent who contributed and tradesmen who provided materials, perhaps for maintenance of the church. Records relating to the maintenance of the poor are also useful. The accounts of the overseers of the poor show who benefited from the monies levied from the parishioners. You may also find the names of those who provided shoes, clothes, fuel or medical care for paupers. In addition, there may be records of pauper apprentices. Parish chest documents might also include those that were created as a result of the settlement legislation, examinations of the mothers of illegitimate children, the accounts of the parish constable and references to highway maintenance.

You may also find vestry minutes for your place. Select or Closed Vestries were small groups of non-elected men who met to discuss parish governance. Open Vestries were rather different and were open to all parishioners. All these documents, where they survive, should be in County Record Offices. Hopefully their catalogue will allow you to identify any that relate to your place. For more information, see Tate, W E *The Parish Chest* (3rd edition Phillimore 2010).

The Oath of Allegiance

Following the Jacobite Rebellion of 1715, there was a resurgence of anti-Catholic feeling. During 1722-1723, all those over eighteen had to swear an oath of allegiance to the crown at their local Quarter Sessions courts. Surviving lists are in County Record Offices. Some have been indexed and are available online.

Ecclesiastical Visitations

These visitations were part of a programme of visits by bishops to the main towns in their diocese, where they would meet with the local clergy. These normally took place every three years. In the eighteenth century, printed series of questions were sent round to the clergy in advance. The questions varied but might include matters relating to population, the frequency of services and communion, schools in the parish and numbers of non-conformists. Churchwardens also had to make presentments of malefactors in their parish.

For example, in 1745, the rector of Menheniot, Cornwall commented in response to the question about schools in the parish, *'There is a school house in the parish not endowed but the master died lately and a new one is but just come. The number of children at present taught is 27. There are some poor children to be taught to read by contribution amounting to £5 yearly'.*

The returns should be in the Diocesan Record Offices.

Gravestones

Gravestones and monuments inside places of worship are an important resource for One Place Studies. Not only do they commemorate those who are buried there but they may also mention residents, or former residents, who were buried elsewhere or who had no burial as their bodies were lost at sea, or in war. The information on gravestones can help to confirm relationships between individuals and may also connect those commemorated to a specific property in your community.

Project - Buried in Your Place

Unless the graveyard is very small, you will need a plan to help with this project. It may be that the Parochial Church Council can provide this for Anglican graveyards. Aim to acquire good quality photographs of all the gravestones and memorials in the churchyards, cemeteries and burial grounds in your place, as well as any monuments inside places of worship. This can be accomplished without professional quality equipment; there should be no necessity to spend more than two hundred pounds on a camera. Getting the best quality pictures does involve squatting down so you are directly opposite each stone but as a rough guide, a reasonably fit person can photograph about eighty gravestones in a session without too many ill effects. The photographs, when enlarged, can be useful for checking transcripts.

Full transcriptions of every readable stone can then be made, don't forget to record such things as the mason's name. This will probably take several sessions as different times of day and weather conditions make some stones easier, or more difficult, to read. You may also have to wait for undergrowth to be cut down or die back in winter. It is easiest to work in pairs, with one person reading and the other writing. The resulting transcripts should then be checked with the original stone, ideally with the other member of the pair reading the stone on that occasion. Be careful to treat the memorials with respect. Scrubbing does not necessarily improve the readability of a stone and should be discouraged as you may be irreparably damaging not just the stone but protected lichens that are growing on it.

If you can cross reference your transcriptions with the burial registers, adding any additional information, this will enhance your resource. You may be surprised at how many discrepancies there are between the information on the stones and that in the burial registers. In addition, you could invite people to submit photographs of any of those that are commemorated, perhaps making contact with descendants through the local paper or the family history network.

Projects such as these can be taken to another level, with graveyards or cemeteries becoming a community resource. Can you create a treasure hunt or trail through your graveyard, encouraging people to look for some of the more unusual stones? It might be possible to put QR codes by certain monuments that will link to your website, where further details about the individuals can be found. Can you link with a local gardeners' club or natural history society to incorporate wildlife or wildflowers in your trail? Can your graveyard and the stories of those who rest there, become an inspiration for local artists or writers? Children could be involved in many aspects of this type of project. Ryde Social Heritage Group have taken this approach and won an award for their project **www.rshg.org.uk/index.asp**.

Note that many graveyards have already been transcribed, or at least had their stones indexed, by local Family History Societies. Do check for such transcripts in local record repositories and libraries and the library of the Society of Genealogists before you begin.

Muster Rolls and Militia Records

Members of the militia were able-bodied men, between the ages of sixteen and sixty, who held themselves in readiness as a local defence force and who were occasionally required to serve outside the immediate area. From 1522-1640 formal inspections, or musters, of these troops were carried out on a regular basis. The resulting Militia Muster Rolls are in The National Archives; their Research Guides *Militia* and *Militia: further research* are useful. Later Muster Rolls might be found in County Record Offices, with the Quarter Sessions' records. For the whereabouts of surviving records see Gibson, Jeremy and Dell, Alan *Tudor and Stuart Muster Rolls* (Federation of Family History Societies 1996) and Gibson, Jeremy and Medlycott, Mervyn *Militia Lists and Musters 1757-1876* (5th edition Family History Partnership 2013). If lists survive for your place, you will have details of the able-bodied men in the area for a specific date, which will complement earlier and later names lists.

Title Deeds and Leases

Title deeds and leases are invaluable for relating inhabitants of your place to specific properties and helping to create residential histories of the dwellings in your community. These records may be in County Record Offices, The National Archives or in private hands. Your chances of locating them will depend on how rigorous the cataloguing is at the archive where they are held. Many repositories have large collections of un-catalogued material and deeds and leases are often amongst them.

In the early eighteenth century, deeds registries were set up for Middlesex (excluding the City of London) and Yorkshire but nothing similar exists for other counties. The Middlesex registers, dating from 1709-1938, are held in The London Metropolitan Archives, see their information leaflet 38. The registries for Yorkshire are divided into Ridings and are held at the appropriate local record office. The following National Archives' Research Guides are useful, *Conveyances of Land for Charitable uses in Trust Deeds 1736-1925* and *Enrolment of Deeds and Registration of Titles to Land*, as is Tim Wormleighton's *Title Deeds for Family Historians* (Family History Partnership 2012).

Records of Apprentices and Freemen

Many towns kept records of apprentices, giving the name of the apprentice, their guardian and the master, together with details of the trade, the term of apprenticeship and the premium paid. There may also be lists of town freemen or burgesses. If your place is a town, you will want to investigate whether or not such records survive in local record repositories. See *My Ancestor was an Apprentice* by Stuart Raymond (Society of Genealogists 2010).

Fire Insurance Records

From the late seventeenth century fire insurance offices were established in London and provincial offices soon followed. Three of the earliest companies are The Hand-in-Hand Fire and Life Insurance Society (established in 1696), the Sun Insurance Office (established in 1710 as Sun Fire) and the Royal Exchange Assurance (established in 1720). Householders, particularly in towns, were keen to insure their properties against fire. The fire-fighting service provided by the insurance companies would only be summoned if the property of one of their policy holders was threatened. Insured properties displayed a fire insurance mark, or plaque, which gave the policy number and indicated that that property was covered. If there are any of these marks remaining on houses or businesses in your place, they are certainly worth further investigation. Unfortunately, fire insurance plaques now have an antique value and may have been attached to the wrong dwelling. Many insured properties will have lost their plaques.

Registers of policy holders are normally arranged by policy number so, unless you have a plaque in situ, it is difficult to access unindexed policy entries. The records normally give the policy number; the name of agent and whereabouts of the agency; the policyholder's name, address, status and occupation; any tenants' names, occupations and addresses; the location, type, nature of construction and value of the insured property; the premium paid and the date that the policy is to be renewed.

The Guildhall Library holds records for about forty London based fire insurance companies, whose policies relate to properties country wide. These include The Sun Fire Office's registers and a county by county index of policy holders for the period 1714-1730, covering English counties but excluding London. For further details see the leaflet available at **www.history.ac.uk/gh/fire.htm**. The Guildhall Library also has microfiche of 150,000 Royal Exchange Assurance and Sun Fire Office policies. There is an index to some Sun Fire Office policy registers at **www.history. ac.uk/gh/sun.htm**. The records of some companies have been deposited in County Record Offices.

For further information see Hawkings, David *Fire Insurance Records for Family and Local Historians* (Francis Boutle Publishers 2003). Cockerell, H A L and Green, Edwin *The British Insurance Business 1547 to 1970* (Heinemann Educational 1976) gives brief details of local holdings. Two research guides *Fire Insurance Records at Guildhall Library* and *A Place in the Sun Index Instructions* can be downloaded from the website of the Guildhall Library **www.cityoflondon.gov.uk/guildhalllibrary**. There is also useful background information on the London Lives website **www.londonlives.org/static/AHDSFIR.jsp**.

Quarter Sessions and other Court Records

Surviving Quarter Sessions' Records might date from the sixteenth century and continue until 1972 but their greatest use for One Place Studies is probably for the eighteenth and nineteenth centuries. The courts are most noted for dealing with minor criminal offences. The records might include depositions, or witness statements; indictment books with names of offenders, their offences and dates of conviction and calendars of prisoners and their sentences. Do not neglect the Petty Sessions Court, which dealt with minor offences. Their records should be in County Record Offices. Assize Courts conducted trials for more serious offences. Their records are held in Classes ASSI1-ASSI77 at The National Archives, with records for earlier than 1559 being in Class JUST3. The following Research Guides are relevant: *Civil Trials in the English Assize Courts 1656-1971: key to records*; *Criminal and Civil Trials in the Welsh Assize Courts 1831-1971: key to records*; *Criminal Trials in the Assize Courts 1559-1971* and *Criminal Trials in the English Assize Courts 1559-1971: key to records*. There may be copies of Assize Calendars held locally.

The Quarter Sessions deal with far more than just crimes. Amongst the many things that you may find are victuallers' licences; lists of insolvent debtors; gamekeepers' certificates; muster rolls; tax returns; coroners' reports; oaths of allegiance by Catholics and Protestant non-conformists. There are also records relating to poor relief, illegitimacy and settlement legislation.[30]

These records are difficult to use for One Place Studies unless they have been indexed, although you may be aware of a criminal case from a newspaper report, which might guide you to the court record. Fortunately, some Quarter Sessions' records have been published. For the survival and whereabouts of Quarter Sessions' records see Gibson, Jeremy *Quarter Sessions Records for Family Historians: a select list* (5th edition Family History Partnership 2007).

For trials at the Central Criminal Court, or Old Bailey, search the website Old Bailey Online **www.oldbaileyonline.org**. Places can be put into the advanced search 'keyword' box and this will bring up mentions of your community for the period 1674-1913.

Project - Crime in Your Place

Use court records and newspapers to study crime and criminals from your place. There are lists of prisoners and bankrupts in the *London Gazette*, which should be searched.[31] If they received custodial sentences, see if relevant prison records survive, as these may contain photographs. If your place contained a prison, bridewell or lock up, an investigation of its history could form part of your research. If any of your inhabitants were transported, you could follow up their story overseas.[32] You could extend this project by also looking for any policemen or parish constables who lived in your location. Most online census image providers allow advanced searches by occupation and place of residence, with no necessity to enter a name.

Further Reading
Alcock, N W *Old Title Deeds* (Phillimore 1986).
Cockerell, H A L and Green, Edwin *The British Insurance Business 1547 to 1970* (Heinemann Educational 1976).

---

[30] See Chapter 7, Parish Chest, p. 50.
[31] See Chapter 6, Newspapers, p. 45.
[32] See Chapter 11, Tracing Migrants, Project - Emigrants, p. 78.

Cornwall, Julian *An Introduction to Reading Old Title Deeds* (Federation of Family History Societies 1993).

Dibben, A A *Title Deeds* (Historical Association 1972).

Gibson, Jeremy *Quarter Sessions Records for Family Historians: a select list* (5th edition Family History Partnership 2007).

Gibson, Jeremy and Dell, Alan *Tudor and Stuart Muster Rolls* (Federation of Family History Societies 1996).

Gibson, Jeremy; Medlycott, Mervyn and Mills, Dennis *Land and Window Tax Assessments* (2nd edition Federation of Family History Societies 1998).

Gibson, Jeremy and Medlycott, Mervyn *Militia Lists and Musters 1757-1876* (5th edition Family History Partnership 2013).

Hawkings, David *Fire Insurance Records for Family and Local Historians* (Francis Boutle Publishers 2003).

The National Archives' Research Guide *Civil Trials in the English Assize Courts 1656-1971: key to records.*

The National Archives' Research Guide *Criminal Trials in the Assize Courts 1559-1971.*

The National Archives' Research Guide *Criminal Trials in the English Assize Courts 1559-1971: key to records.*

The National Archives' Research Guide *Criminal and Civil Trials in the Welsh Assize Courts 1831-1971: key to records.*

The National Archives' Research Guide *Manors.*

The National Archives' Research Guide *Manors: further research.*

The National Archives' Research Guide *Militia.*

The National Archives' Research Guide *Militia: further research.*

The National Archives' Research Guide *Using the Manorial Documents Register and how to find Manorial Lordships.*

Park, Peter *My Ancestors Were Manorial Tenants: how can I find out more about them?* (Society of Genealogists 1994).

Raymond, Stuart *My Ancestor was an Apprentice* (Society of Genealogists 2010).

Stuart, Denis *Manorial Records: an introduction to their transcription and translation* (Phillimore 1992).

Tate, W E *The Parish Chest* (3rd edition Phillimore 2010).

Western, J R *The English Militia in the Eighteenth Century: the story of a political issue 1660-1802* (Routledge and Kegan Paul 1965).

Wormleighton, Tim *Title Deeds for Family Historians* (Family History Partnership 2012).

Chapter Eight

The Seventeenth Century

Protestation Oath Rolls

The Protestation Oath Rolls, or Protestation Returns, were created in 1641/1642. The signatories were confirming a belief in the Protestant religion, allegiance to the king and support for the rights and privileges of Parliament. There are suggestions that some individuals signed twice, perhaps in their home parish and again in the nearest market town. With a few exceptions, notably Cornwall, most returns were compiled by officials so do not contain actual signatures.

The majority of the original Returns are in the Parliamentary Archives, at the Palace of Westminster, arranged by county and sub-divided into hundreds[33] and parishes. Rolls survive for about a third of English counties, forming a virtual census of all males aged eighteen and over; there are also a few female names. There are a handful of locally held returns and occasional copied lists in parish registers. For details of the areas for which returns survive, the whereabouts of the originals and the existence of transcripts, see Gibson, Jeremy and Dell, Alan *Protestation Returns 1641-42 and other Contemporary Listings* (Family History Partnership 2009). The guide *Family History Resources at the Parliamentary Archives*, which can be downloaded from **www.parliament.uk**, gives more information. For links to online transcripts of the returns see **edwardvallance.files.wordpress.com/2011/06/ on-line protestationreturns.pdf**, although this does not seem to be up to date.

There were similar oaths of loyalty to Parliament and the Protestant church taken in 1643, 'The Vow and Covenant' and 'The Solemn League and Covenant'. Although these were national oaths, the records are not held centrally and very few survive. Some are listed in Gibson, Jeremy and Dell, Alan *Protestation Returns 1641-42 and other Contemporary Listings* (Family History Partnership 2009) but this is not a comprehensive list of these particular documents.

Collection for Distressed Protestants in Ireland 1641/2

A rebellion by Irish Catholics, objecting to the deliberate 'planting' of English Protestant settlers, led to the massacre of thousands of Protestants. Charles I ordered each parish to collect money to help put down the rebellion and provide relief for the refugees, who had fled to the safety of the English held garrison towns, or to England itself.

Surviving lists of subscribers, arranged by county and hundred, are in Classes E179 and SP28 at The National Archives. Occasionally, parishes made their own lists that

---

[33] A hundred is an ancient administrative unit into which counties or shires were divided.

survive locally, perhaps copied in to the parish register. For details of the whereabouts of the returns, see Gibson, Jeremy and Dell, Alan *The Protestation Returns 1641-42 and other Contemporary Listings* (Family History Partnership 2009).

Hearth Tax

The Hearth Tax was levied between 1662 and 1689, although records survive to 1674 only. Anyone who was occupying a house that was worth more than £1 a year had to pay two shillings for each hearth. Those with less valuable properties and anyone in receipt of poor relief were exempt. Some lists of exemptions also survive, so the more complete returns can act as a census of heads of household. Not only do these records allow you to find out who was living in your place at this particular time but their relative wealth can be discovered by comparing the number of hearths.

The original Hearth Tax Returns, made by the parish constable and submitted to the Justices of the Peace at the Lady Day and Michaelmas Quarter Sessions, are held at The National Archives; their Research Guide *Taxation before 1689* is useful. Lottery funding has enabled The University of Roehampton to provide local record offices with microfilm copies of the centrally held returns for their area. A few contemporary copies have been retained with Quarter Sessions' records and are therefore held locally.

Transcriptions of many Hearth Tax Returns are now available. Details of the survival and whereabouts of original records, in The National Archives and elsewhere, together with information about transcripts, can be found in Gibson, Jeremy *Hearth Tax Returns, other Later Stuart Tax Lists and the Association Oath Rolls* (2nd edition Federation of Family History Societies 1996). The website Hearth Tax Online **www.hearthtax.org.uk** gives details of all the returns that have been transcribed by The Centre for Hearth Tax Research. The website also contains statistical maps and lists all published returns. The British Record Society **www.british recordsociety.org**, in conjunction with the University of Roehampton, have a publishing programme aimed at producing a series of county volumes of Hearth Tax returns. Copies are available from The British Record Society.

Hearth Tax Returns can be used as population indicators for your place. Historians have debated the precise relationship between the number of individuals listed in the returns and the total population but the generally held view is that multiplying by 4·3 will give a reasonably reliable figure.[34]

Seventeenth Century Poll Taxes

Seven poll taxes were raised between 1660 and 1697. In this period, poll taxes sometimes listed not just heads of household but also family members and servants. Sadly not many of these records survive but those that do are in County Record Offices. There are some lists of defaulters in The National Archives. For details, consult The National Archives' E179 database **www.nationalarchives.gov.uk/ E179**. A county to county guide to the survival and whereabouts of these records is Jeremy Gibson's *The Hearth Tax, Other Later Stuart Tax Lists and the Association Oath Rolls* (2nd edition Federation of Family History Societies 1996).

Compton's Census

In 1676, the numbers of Anglican communicants, known as 'conformists', Protestant dissenters and Catholics were recorded. The resulting ecclesiastical census takes its name from Henry Compton, the then Bishop of London. In many instances all those aged sixteen and over were automatically counted as 'conformists'. Some returns are believed to erroneously include under sixteens as well, others appear to have only counted males.

The returns are arranged by parish, arch-deaconry and diocese. For the areas that are covered, the Midlands, Wales and the South of England, estimated populations and the extent of non-conformity can be gleaned. With the exception of nineteen parishes, for which more detailed returns survive, names of individual residents are not listed. See Gibson, Jeremy and Medlycott, Mervyn *Local Census Listings 1522-1930 - Holdings in the British Isles* (3rd edition Federation of Family History Societies 1998) for details of the survival and whereabouts of these records. There are copies at The William Salt Library, Stafford **www.staffordshire.gov.uk/leisure/ archives/williamsalt/home.aspx** and The Bodleian Library, Oxford **www. bodleian. ox.ac.uk.** Whiteman Annie (ed.) *The Compton Census of 1676: a critical edition* (Oxford University Press 1986) is a full transcription of the census. Even for areas where no names are recorded, this is a useful source for getting an impression of the extent of non-conformity in your place.

Association Oath Rolls

This was an oath of loyalty to the crown, taken in 1695/6. The originals for England and Wales are in Class C213 in The National Archives. This oath was taken by men of some standing in the community, such as office holders and clergy. The oath was certainly taken in Scotland and probably in Ireland but there are no centrally held surviving records. There may be some fragments in private archives or burgh records.

---

[34] Arkell, Tom 'Multiplying Factors for Estimating Population Totals from the Hearth Tax' in *Local Population Studies* 28 1982 pp. 51-57.

See Gibson, Jeremy *Hearth Tax Returns, other Later Stuart Tax Lists and the Association Oath Rolls* (2nd edition Federation of Family History Societies 1996), for details of survival rates.

Project - Seventeenth Century Surnames Survey[35]

Most of the sources for this century are lists of names that are rarely linked with a specific dwelling. Nonetheless a combination of the above records can be used to look at the surnames that are associated with your place in the seventeenth century. Try to be aware of which are distinct surnames and which are spelling variants of what is intrinsically the same name. If parish registers survive for this period the information from these can be added. The survey can also be extended earlier and later, using other lists of names.

Seventeenth Century Surnames Survey[35]

Record	Stapleton and variants	Heal and varients
Earliest Parish Register Entry	Stapleton 1603	Heale 1611
Protestation Return	Stapelton	Heal Heale Hele
Distressed Protestants	Stapelton	Heal
Hearth Tax	Stapleton Stapledon	Heal
1694 Poll Tax	None Listed	Heale
Latest Parish Register Entry	Stapledon 1687	Heal 1693

Further Reading

Arkell, Tom 'Multiplying Factors for Estimating Population Totals from the Hearth Tax' in *Local Population Studies* 28 1982 pp. 51-57.

Gibson, Jeremy *Hearth Tax Returns, other Later Stuart Tax Lists and the Association Oath Rolls* (2nd edition Federation of Family History Societies 1996).

Gibson, Jeremy and Dell, Alan *The Protestation Returns 1641-42 and other contemporary listings* (Family History Partnership 2009).

Gibson, Jeremy and Medlycott, Mervyn *Local Census Listings 1522-1930 - Holdings in the British Isles* (3rd edition Federation of Family History Societies 1998).

The National Archives' Research Guide *Taxation before 1689.*

The National Archives' Research Guide *Oaths of Loyalty to the Crown and Church of England.*

Whiteman Annie (ed.) *The Compton Census of 1676: a critical edition* (Oxford University Press 1986).

---

[35] Unlike most of the examples in this book, this survey is fictitious and illustrates a place with an unusual wealth of surviving records.

Chapter Nine

Before 1600

Early Sources

If you are researching in the sixteenth century, or earlier, documents are frequently very difficult to read and might well be in Latin. For this reason, some people undertaking One Place Studies are reluctant to extend their research back into the Medieval era. It is however an important time for lists of the first surnames in your community. These should not be neglected, especially now increasing numbers of early documents are being transcribed and made available online, thus reducing the access difficulties. This period also sees the beginning of vital mainstream sources such as wills, parish registers and leases. Two useful general websites for this period are **medievalgenealogy.org.uk** and **www.manuscriptsonline.org**. The National Archives' Research Guide *Medieval and Early Modern Family History* is useful. See also Franklin, Peter *Some Medieval Records for Family Historians* (Federation of Family History Societies 1994).

Domesday Survey

The Domesday Survey was commissioned by William I in 1086. The survey is arranged by hundred. There were two volumes, one covering Essex, Norfolk and Suffolk and the other for most of the rest of the country. Cumberland, Durham, Northumberland, northern Westmorland, London and Winchester are not included. The Bolden Book, drawn up c. 1183, covered Northumberland and Durham. The National Archives hold the original Domesday manuscript; there is background information in their Research Guide *Domesday Book*. Colour facsimiles of Domesday entries can be downloaded from The National Archives' 'Discovery' catalogue, for a small fee. See also Williams, Ann and Martin, G H (ed.) *Domesday Book: a complete translation* (Viking/Allen Lane 2003).

The Domesday Book Online website **www.domesdaybook.co.uk** can be searched by place name. There are also links to opportunities to purchase, rather expensive, facsimiles. This site is valuable for the historical background it provides but a better option for acquiring details of your place is Open Domesday **www.domesdaymap.co.uk**. This allows for searches by modern place name or postcode. Free facsimiles can be downloaded and used, with certain copyright provisos.

Poll Taxes, Lay Subsidies and Other Taxes

Tax lists exist from the twelfth century. Most of these records are in The National Archives, primarily in Class E179. The Research Guide *Taxation before 1689* is relevant. A database, containing descriptions of all the documents in E179, can be searched at **www.nationalarchives.gov.uk/E179**. The documents are indexed by place, tax or year but not by personal name. Included in this database are fifteenths and tenths, which were a form of taxation in force from 1134-1624. Many of the assessments for 1332 have been printed and can be accessed using British History Online **www.british-history.ac.uk**. Be aware that most of the fifteenths and tenths records list places and amount payable but not personal names. They can still be used to compare the wealth of your place with others in the area. There are no returns for the counties of Cheshire and Durham, which were exempt.

Lay subsidies were a tax on the laity, as opposed to the clergy. The resulting documents list wealthier members of the community. The earliest subsidy rolls do not list names. The so-called 'Great Subsidy', raised in 1524-1527, is the most useful. The last subsidies were collected in the mid seventeenth century. Some records have been published. The website **www.british-history.ac.uk** gives access to some returns; individual transcripts are available on other websites. The lists that include names are often the earliest records of particular surnames being present in your place.

Inquisitions Post Mortem

These are, literally, 'enquiries after death', conducted following the death of someone who held Crown land. The records span the period 1236-1646 and describe the land holdings and heirs of the deceased. The records, which are in Latin, are at The National Archives, primarily in Classes C132-C142. See their Research Guide *Landholders and Heirs in Inquisitions Post Mortem 1236-c.1640*, for further information. Unfortunately many of the records are searchable by county and not smaller place but it would be worth searching under some of the prominent surnames that are known to have been in your community in the medieval period. There are published Calendars of Inquisitions for the periods 1235-1392 and 1485-1509. Some local record societies have printed the inquisitions for their area.

Pipe Rolls

These Exchequer documents consist of accounts recording the income of the crown. Originally, they were known as 'The Great Roll of the Exchequer'. The name 'pipe roll' is taken from their appearance. They are held at The National Archives in Class E372, with the copy 'Chancellor's Rolls' in E352. The Research Guide *Early Pipe Rolls 1130-c.1300* is a useful introduction. This series of records go back further than any other, with a continuous run from 1155-1832 and an earlier roll for 1129-1130. They are arranged by county but beyond that it may be difficult to identify entries that specifically relate to your place. They are however a useful source of early names[36] and might be useful when used in connection with other sources. Outstanding debts were carried forward from year to year so some entries might be out of date.

The records are in Latin until 1733 and the abbreviated script, used from about

---

[36]   In the early rolls they are likely to be by-names, rather than hereditary surnames.

1300, means that the earliest rolls can be easier to decipher than those of the seventeenth century. Dealing with this class of record in its original form can be daunting but many of the twelfth and thirteenth century rolls have been transcribed, indexed and published by the Pipe Roll Society **www.piperollsociety.co.uk**. Information from some of these records can also be found at **www.british-history.ac.uk**.

Feet of Fines

These documents, dating from 1182-1833, are records of land transfer, which took place by means of a, usually fictitious, court case. The agreement was written three times on a piece of parchment and divided by cutting a wavy or indented line. The two top sections were written side by side and were kept by the parties involved. The third copy, at the 'foot' of the document, was filed with the Court of Common Pleas and is now at The National Archives, principally in Class CP25. Unfortunately there is no personal or place index for these documents and the early fines are in Latin, making this a difficult class of record to use. At present, only those that have been printed and indexed are going to be usable; see Kissock, Jonathan 'Medieval Feet of Fines: a study of their uses with a catalogue of published sources' in *Local Historian* 24 1994 pp. 66-82. Some of the older texts listed by Kissock are available at **www.archive.org/details/texts**. The National Archives' Research Guide, *Land Conveyances: feet of fines, 1182-1833* is useful.

Chancery Courts

Records of the Court of Chancery are held by The National Archives in Class C. They date from the fourteenth to the nineteenth century and include disputes over such things as inheritance, land ownership and debts. For this reason they can be useful for One Place Studies because they may help with reconstructing families and linking individuals to particular properties. Relevant National Archives' Research Guides are *Chancery Proceedings: equity suits before 1558*; *Chancery Proceedings: equity suits from 1558* and *Chancery Cases in the Supreme Court after 1875*. Place searches, using The National Archives' 'Discovery' Catalogue, are often more successful than name searches in this class of record.

Wills

Wills for the inhabitants of your place can be very useful, particularly if property formed part of their bequests. The problem is finding the relevant probate material. For wills proved post January 1858, when they are in the keeping of the Principal Probate Registry, this is very difficult. You may well be limited to working from burial records and looking up residents on an individual basis. Even before this date, success will depend on the indexing of wills by the appropriate County Record Office; many will be indexed by name rather than abode. To discover where wills for the residents of your community might be held at this time see Humphery-Smith, Cecil R (ed.)

Phillimore Atlas and Index of Parish Registers (3rd edition Phillimore 2003) or Gibson, Jeremy and Churchill, Else *Probate Jurisdictions: where to look for wills* (5th edition Federation of Family History Societies 2002). Ideally you will be able to collect information about extant wills from family historians who have researched the inhabitants of your community.

The National Wills Index, for pre 1858 wills, can be searched by name at **www.origins.net**. There are also some county wills indexes that can be searched by place. One series of wills that it is possible to search by place is those proved in the Prerogative Court of Canterbury (PCC), which are held by The National Archives. These include testators from all over the country, although there is a tendency towards the wills of the more affluent or non-conformists. Using the 'Discovery' catalogue of The National Archives, all the PCC wills for residents of your place can be identified and downloaded for a small fee.

Parish Registers

Parish registers, detailing baptisms, marriages and burials, are one of the key building blocks of your One Place Study. The earliest registers might date from 1538, although many sixteenth century registers do not survive. Apart from the most recent registers, the records should now be in the County Record Office. There are an increasing number of parish registers that are indexed and available online, frequently via subscription websites. Whilst these are useful for family history, they are less so for One Place Studies. A One Place Study requires a complete, chronological coverage that is really only available from a full transcription or access to images of the original registers in page order.

Looking at the register as a whole, rather than at entries relating to a particular family, allows you to be aware of gaps in the records or idiosyncrasies of the particular parish clerk. For example if pre 1813 burials of infants are normally noted as such, you might suspect that entries, in the same handwriting, that are not so annotated, relate to older people. A page by page study of the registers will also reveal any additional comments that may have been recorded, such as references to extreme weather events, epidemics, the collapse of the church tower or the arrival of a new incumbent.

If your place is a single parish, or consists of more than one whole parish, you will almost certainly aim to transcribe all the parish registers and probably put them into a database, so that they can be searched by name or abode. If your place is a part of a parish, the use of parish registers is more difficult. Later registers may give explicit enough addresses for the inhabitants of your hamlet or street to be identified but this will be impossible for earlier centuries. More detailed registers, with standard information, begin in 1754 for marriages and 1813 for baptisms and burials. By the twentieth century, church registers give a much less complete picture and many children are not baptised, marriages take place in register offices, or not at all and burials are in cemeteries, or are replaced by cremations.

If parish registers are missing, you might use the Bishops' Transcripts, a second copy of the register entries that was sent annually to the bishop. They date from 1598 and are rare beyond the mid nineteenth century. Survival is patchy; see Gibson, Jeremy *Bishops' Transcripts and Marriage Licences, Bonds and Allegations: a guide to their location and indexes* (6th edition Family History Partnership 2013) for details. Even if your parish registers survive, it is a good idea to seek out Bishops' Transcripts as sometimes they contain additional, or slightly different, entries to the registers.

If your place is in a northern English county, you may be lucky and find that it adopted the more detailed register format instigated by Bishop Dade for the period 1777-1812. This means that baptism entries might include date of birth, position in the family, mother's maiden name and the parishes of origin of the parents. If this is the case, you have far greater scope for possible parish register projects for your place.

Apart from their use for discovering the names of the inhabitants of your community, parish registers, particularly more recent ones, have a variety of applications for One Place Studies.

Project - Age at Marriage

Using the post 1837 marriage registers, conduct a survey of the age at which men and women married. Does their occupation or social status make a difference? If you have reconstructed the families in your place and can therefore approximate the ages of brides and grooms from baptism, burial or census records, it may be possible to extend this survey to the period before 1837. This project is made more difficult if 'full age' or 'under age' are habitually used, rather than precise ages.

Project - Literacy

Historians have long argued about the connection between the ability to sign one's name in a marriage register and the possession of a functional level of literacy. It is also known that someone might sign their name at the time of a first marriage but not subsequently; suggesting that not all those who could sign their names always did so. This does not mean that marriage registers from 1754 cannot be used to study comparative levels of literacy in your place at different times. It is interesting to see what difference the advent of compulsory education makes and how class, gender or occupation impacts on the ability to sign one's name. It is not sensible to include witnesses' names in these surveys, as there are often 'professional' witnesses, frequently the parish clerk, who signed for multiple marriages.

Project - Longevity and Infant Mortality

Once your parish clerk begins to record age at death in the burial registers, certainly from 1813 but if you are lucky, earlier, you can study longevity and infant mortality. What percentage of the burials in your place were for those under five, or over eighty, or indeed any age in between? What impact does gender have? As suggested in Chapter Three, even when ages are not recorded, you can look at numbers of burials in each year to identify peaks that may indicate epidemics.

Heralds' Visitations

Between 1530 and 1686, heralds were required to check that all those using a coat of arms were entitled to do so. Their tours of inspection occurred roughly once in a generation. They referred back to previous visitations, inspected church monuments, stained glass windows and engraved items before assessing a gentleman's claim. Any unlawfully displayed arms, on parchment, plate, memorials or elsewhere, could be defaced or destroyed. The resulting visitation pedigrees will provide evidence for the armigerous residents, or gentry, of your place. The Harleian Society **http:// harleian.org.uk** has published copies of many visitations. Some of these have been made available on CD by S and N Genealogy Supplies **www.genealogysupplies .com**. Be aware that most of the Harleian visitations are based on copies from the British Library rather than the originals, which are at The College of Arms. Some of their 'visitations' volumes are not quite what they seem.

Further Reading

Connolly, Philomena *Maynooth Research Guides for Irish Local History: Medieval record sources* (Four Courts Press 2002).

Franklin, Peter *Some Medieval Records for Family Historians* (Federation of Family History Societies 1994).

Gibson, Jeremy *Bishops' Transcripts and Marriage Licences, Bonds and Allegations: a guide to their location and indexes* (6th edition Family History Partnership 2013).

Gibson, Jeremy and Churchill, Else *Probate Jurisdictions: where to look for wills* (5th edition Federation of Family History Societies 2002).

Grannum, Karen and Taylor, Nigel *Wills and Probate Records: a guide for family historians* (2nd edition The National Archives 2009).

Hallum, M *Domesday Book through Nine Centuries* (Thames and Hudson 1986).

Humphery-Smith, Cecil R (ed.) *Phillimore Atlas and Index of Parish Registers* (3rd edition Phillimore 2003).

Kissock, Jonathan 'Medieval Feet of Fines: a study of their uses with a catalogue of published sources' in *Local Historian* 24 1994 pp. 66-82.

The National Archives' Research Guide *Chancery Cases in the Supreme Court after 1875.*

The National Archives' Research Guide *Chancery Proceedings: equity suits before 1558.*

The National Archives' Research Guide *Chancery Proceedings: equity suits from 1558.*

The National Archives' Research Guide *Death Duties 1796-1903*.

The National Archives' Research Guide *Domesday Book*.

The National Archives' Research Guide *Land Conveyances by Feet of Fines 1182-1833*.

The National Archives' Research Guide *Looking for Records of a Will or Administration after 1858*.

The National Archives' Research Guide *Medieval and Early Modern Family History*.

The National Archives' Research Guide *Wills 1384-1858*.

The National Archives' Research Guide *Wills and Probate: further research*.

Probert, Rebecca *Marriage Law for Genealogists: the definitive guide* (Takeaway Publishing 2012).

Raymond, Stuart *Parish Registers: a history and guide* (Family History Partnership 2009).

Raymond, Stuart *The Wills of our Ancestors* (Pen and Sword 2013).

Williams, Ann and Martin, G H (ed.) *Domesday Book: a complete translation* (Viking/Allen Lane 2003).

Chapter Ten

Tomorrow's History

The history of your community is constantly evolving. You are in a prime position to ensure that this history is kept up to date. It is a good idea to note any significant events that effect your place, perhaps on a monthly basis. If you keep such a record, you will need to decide what to include and how detailed the entries on your list might be. Items that you may consider worth noting are:

Building or demolition work.

The opening or closing of shops and businesses.

The founding or demise of clubs and societies.

Extreme weather events.

Inhabitants' awards and notable achievements.

Comings and goings e.g. the arrival or departure of a new head teacher, vicar or chairman of the parish council.

Major social events: perhaps not each meeting of every club and society but occasions such as the annual parish fete, carnival or jubilee celebrations.

Births, marriages and deaths. If you record these there may be privacy implications, so consider how you use the information.

A good way to keep abreast of what is going on is to monitor local newspapers for references to your place, keeping any relevant cuttings. Free newsletters are frequently circulated within a community and are also very helpful. Monitoring history as it happens is easier if you are a resident of your place but it is certainly not impossible from a distance. You may be able to find someone local who will help, or you could subscribe to newspapers and newsletters, many of which have online versions. A good community website will also have information that could be helpful in this respect. The website of the relevant local authority will enable you to access any planning applications that relate to your area. Many applications are turned down and not all those that are granted permission come to fruition. It is those that are carried out that are most significant for your One Place Study.

Maintaining an ongoing pictorial record is also important. Photographs of buildings, people and events taken today will be an invaluable historical resource for the future. Gathering estate agents' details, as suggested in Chapter Two, is a good way of obtaining current images of the interior and exterior of properties.

Project - Today's Census

It is possible to attempt census-like snapshots of your community at a particular point in time. Some towns and villages used the millennium or the Queen's Jubilee as the impetus for such an activity but it does not need to be associated with a national event. Such projects range from a simple list of who lived where on a specific date, to something much more detailed. Inhabitants can be invited to submit photographs of themselves outside their properties, together with mini-biographies, or, if you are local, you could offer to take the photographs yourself. Attractive though this idea sounds, there are inherent difficulties when dealing with the present. Many people, quite understandably, may not wish to take part in such a project. The way in which the information is used also needs careful thought. Sometimes such photographs and biographies are displayed in village halls or other community buildings. Although this creates a wonderful historic record, it does publicise the names and whereabouts of young children and also makes it clear where elderly people are living alone.

A way of overcoming some of these issues and gaining support for a project such as this, might be to market it as a time capsule. The information and photographs could be collected with the agreement that they would not be publicised for a specified period. Even a five year time delay might be enough to allay fears and persuade a reasonable number of residents to co-operate. If there is a reluctance to participate on an individual footing, maybe you could encourage the inhabitants of a particular road to contribute a group picture for their street. You might also persuade local institutions to take part, providing photographs of current members. In this way, you will have a record of the local football team or the Women's Institute at your chosen moment in time. This will complement the individual records and is especially valuable if people are hesitant about contributing on a personal basis.

This project is clearly much more difficult to administer if you do not live in your place, or if your study area is very large. It is still possible to accomplish something along these lines, perhaps by inviting people to upload pictures and information to a website or Facebook group. Do make sure that participants are well aware of privacy issues and implications. As there will be no time delay in this case, it may be preferable to limit your project to group and society pictures.

Part Three
Pulling it All Together

Chapter Eleven
Making Connections

Why Bother?

There comes a point when you need to begin to collate and integrate the data that you have collected. There is a temptation to delay this stage, on the grounds that there is always one more class of document to index, or one more source to transcribe. It is however important to begin some form of cohesive record sooner rather than later. Firstly, delay can mean that the accumulation of information makes attempting any kind of synthesis seem daunting. Secondly, much of your information may be in the form of transcriptions or spreadsheets, which do not have an intrinsic fascination, especially for a non-specialist audience. Narratives, stories and illustrations, that are the end product of pulling your material together, are more appealing for the general public than lists and databases. Some form of coherent 'publication',[37] in the widest sense of the word, is the best possible way to generate interest in your One Place Study and thereby gain further information.

Your research moves from being a collection of data to a true One Place Study when you begin to make connections, between individuals, between inhabitants and locations and between people, places and events. In this way, you gain an insight into the lives of past residents and shed light on issues such as household composition, occupational structure, migration patterns and residential persistence. This chapter suggests some of the ways in which this might be done.

Linking People

The ubiquitous parish reconstitutions, beloved of The Cambridge Group[38] of demographers, make links between various records that ostensibly refer to the same person. These often depend heavily on parish registers and tend to concentrate on the period prior to 1837. Some researchers in this field are greatly reliant on computer algorithms to make these connections; connections which might have genealogists throwing their hands up in horror. The dictionary definition of 'reconstitution' is '*a fresh constitution*'.[39] This suggests that something is being added that was not part

---

[37] See Chapter 12.
[38] The Cambridge Group for the History of Population and Social Structure
www.geog.cam.ac.uk/research/centres/campop.
[39] *Oxford English Dictionary.*

of the original ingredients. An alternative and perhaps preferable, term is 'recon-struction', described as *'restoring something past'*,[40] a much more laudable aim.

Ruth Finnegan wrote that, in order to understand a community, 'we need to move beyond individual people or families to study relationships between them.'[41] Although the largest One Place Studies might find this impractical, most will aim to link inhabitants together in a series of family trees. There are plenty of books on tracing family history[42] and many of the necessary sources have been mentioned in earlier chapters; so this is not the place for a detailed description of how to build up a pedigree. Tracing the family histories of all the people who lived in your place may seem overwhelming but it is usually possible to enlist help. There will be family historians working on many of these families. It is a good idea to join the Family History Society[43] that covers your community and make use of their members' interests' lists, message boards, Facebook groups and other means of communication. Normally these are designed to facilitate contact between those interested in the same surname but it is usually possible to use them to identify researchers with ancestors who came from your place. Exchanging information can be mutually beneficial and will provide you with family trees and biographical details relating to the past residents of your community. The usual provisos apply to information gathered in this way. It will only be as good as the researcher who supplied it and should be checked for accuracy.

Most family tree software will allow you to add a series of unrelated trees to the same file. This is important for a One Place Study, when you may subsequently find ways to link the pedigrees of single families. In most communities, many of the pre twentieth century residents will be related in some verifiable way. Once you have the basis of your composite community family tree, you can begin to study the kinship links between the inhabitants of your place.

Project - Kinship Webs

Investigate the relationships between the heads of household in your community at a particular point in time. This is usually done by using one of the census returns as a basis but you could attempt a similar exercise using a Hearth Tax Return,[44] Land Tax[45] or other list of names. If you are using the census, you will be able to include the spouses of the heads of household, which will give a clearer picture of the kinship web in your place. Discover how each family unit is related to the other households in your community and illustrate the interrelationships. Your family tree software may

---

[40] *Oxford English Dictionary*.
[41] Finnegan, Ruth 'Community: what is it and how can we investigate it?' in Pryce, W T R *From Family History to Community History* (Cambridge University Press 1994) p. 209.
[42] See the Bibliography at the end of this volume.
[43] A list of most but not all, UK family history societies can be found at **www.ffhs.org.uk**.
[44] See Chapter 8, p. 58.   [45] See Chapter 7, p. 49.

work out the relationship between two individuals for you. If you have a large One Place Study, you could limit this project to a street or hamlet within your place. In order to carry out this project, you will need to decide what you mean by 'related'. Researchers often distinguish between degrees of kinship. Parents and children or siblings are said to be related in the first degree. Grandparents and grandchildren, uncles/aunts and nephews/nieces, or first cousins, are second degree relationships. Most researchers will stop at this point. It is certainly too involved to take this exercise any further than relationships of the third degree.[46] Beyond this, almost everyone in a rural nineteenth century community will be related.

In close knit communities you may find that two households are related in more than one way; the heads or their spouses may, for example, be both first cousins and second cousins. The usual way to deal with this is to use the closest relationship.

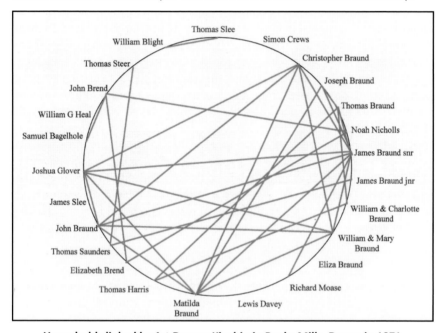

Households linked by 1st Degree Kinship in Bucks Mills, Devon in 1871

In a community where the kinship webs are less complex than Bucks Mills, you could include all three degrees of kinship on one diagram, using colour to distinguish between the different levels of relationship. This type of investigation works best if you repeat the exercise for different points in time and see if the kinship webs remain the same, or become more or less dense. You may be surprised by how much they change. It is also more meaningful if you can compare your findings with those for other communities.

---

[46] Third degree relationships are: great grandparents and great grandchildren, second cousins, great uncles/aunts and great nephews/nieces, first cousins once removed.

People and Places

Another aspect of a One Place Study is linking people to places. This involves trying to compile residential histories for as many of the dwellings in your community as possible. Like several other aspects of One Place Study research, this is often easiest for the period for which census returns are available. Even then, associating people with a specific property is difficult if the address merely reads 'village'. If you are able to relate residents to a particular house, you can begin to consider why they may have moved in or out. Does their change of abode coincide with marriage or the death of a spouse? Do properties pass between members of the same family?

Project - Residential Histories

Using as wide a range of sources as possible, create a spreadsheet for the properties in your place, showing the names of the occupants at specific dates. Some sources give owners rather than occupiers, so be aware of this. Even occupiers, as listed in the Land Tax or Tithe Schedule for example, may sub-let. If your study area is too large for this to be a practical proposition, opt for a street or hamlet within your place. Can you suggest reasons why changes in ownership have taken place? For instance, in the Buckland Brewer example it may be that Ann Moyse is William's widow.

	1832 Land Tax	1841 Census	1841 Tithe Schedule	1851 Census
Bell Cottage	Hannah Dennis	Nicholas Sanders	Nicholas Sanders	Nicholas Sanders
Churchgate Cottage	William Moyse	William Moyse	Ann Moyse	John Short
Castle Cottage	Jeremiah Caddy	William Norman	William Norman	James Abbott
Hills	Robert Clarke	Sarah Johns	Sarah Short	Maria Lee
The Cottage	?	unoccupied	John Pidlar	John Norman

An Extract from Residential Histories in Buckland Brewer, Devon.

Project - Dynastic Families

Lists of names at specific dates can also be used to see how many distinct surnames are present in your place at different times. It is usual to find that the number increases as you come closer to the present. If the population of your place changes significantly, you need to take account of this by calculating the number of different surnames as a percentage of the total population, or estimated population.

Identify the dynastic families in your place, those who persist over many decades and whose members form a large percentage of your community's population. You will probably find that members of these families were at the heart of the kinship webs that you have created in the earlier project.

Projects involving surnames often appeal to primary school children. Those whose families have been in the community for many years are excited to see their own name in the records such as parish registers, school admissions' registers or on the war memorial. Those who are new to the area or even the country can investigate the meanings and origins of their own names. Software such as Steve Archer's Surname Atlas **www.archersoftware.co.uk** is useful here.

Project - Residential Persistence

It is interesting to see how long individuals and families have remained in your place. There are various ways in which you can investigate this. Use a range of documents to track when a particular surname was present in your place. Parish registers are particularly useful in this respect but you can also draw on tax lists, census returns and indeed any source that relates a surname to a place at a specific date. You are looking for a continuous presence in your community. A surname may appear in 1680 and again in 1880 but if there are no references in between, it would be inaccurate to suggest that this family have been residents for 200 years.

Families who remain in Bulkworthy for more than 100 years

It is also possible to look at residential persistence on an individual level. Like many of the suggestions in this book, if you have a large One Place Study, this is a project that might be limited to a small part of your community. One way of doing this is to take a cohort of residents, for example all those in the 1841 census who are ten years old or less. Track these individuals through subsequent censuses to see how many are present in your community for one, two, three, four or more enumerations. If you study another cohort of this age group, starting with the 1881 census, do a similar percentage remain for four enumerations, in other words consistently until 1911? You can further refine this research to see if males and females have comparable levels of persistence or if the social class[47] or occupation of the individuals makes a difference.

---

[47] See Chapter 3 for information about analysis by social class.

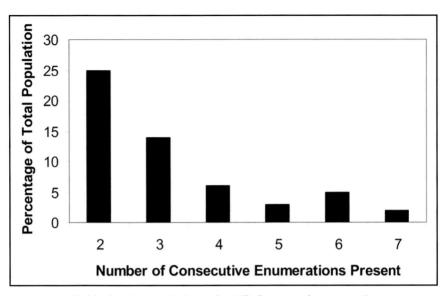

Individuals who remain in Bucks Mills for several enumerations

There is more that can be done to connect individuals and places. Having related people to homes, can you link them to workplaces, schools, places of worship or clubs and associations within your community?

Tracing Migrants

Many of your community's residents will not have spent their whole life there. It helps to understand your own neighbourhood if you examine the inhabitants' relationship with other places as well. Think about what might be going on in your study area that attracts incomers, or results in waves of out-migration. Barry Reay's comment, 'one of the weaknesses of family reconstitution is that it misses the mobile sections of the population,' needs to be addressed.[48] So, part of a One Place Study may involve researching those who arrive and leave and why they may have done so.

It is only feasible to get anything approaching a complete picture of migration patterns during the time when census returns are available. It might be possible to identify in-migrations by racial, ethnic and religious groups such as Huguenots, Jews or West Indians, at other times but only the censuses will provide a more comprehensive record of the movement of named individuals in and out of your community.

Identifying in-migrants is relatively easy. At a basic level, you look at the birthplaces given in the census returns and consider how many residents were born in your community, how many were born elsewhere and how far they have travelled. The results can be depicted in graphs and migration routes can be plotted on maps. It is also interesting to see if the pattern changes during the period for which census

---

[48]   Reay, Barry *Microhistories Demography, Society and Culture in Rural England, 1800-1930* (Cambridge 1966), p. xxi.

returns are available. Be aware though that what you are comparing is their place of birth with their current residence in your community. Many of these in-migrants will have arrived in your community from their birthplace via intermediate places. Tracing every step in a series of migrations is not easy. Each migrant has to be tracked individually and even then, their place of residence between the decennial censuses might only be revealed if they had children born in the intervening locations. Even so, it is more accurate to establish the distance between their most recent previous residence and your community, rather than using birthplaces.

Project - In-Migrants

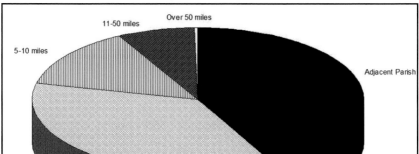

Bulkworthy, Devon in-migrants 1841-1901

Using the birthplace column of the 1851 census returns, create a graph, such as that for Bulkworthy. You may need a Gazetteer to identify some of the birthplaces, or you can use a website such as Google Maps **maps.google.co.uk/maps** or the AA Routeplanner **www.theaa.com/route-planner/index**. These sites will tell you distances between places but remember that these are distances along modern roads. Use these if you wish, or alternatively get a map and a ruler out and measure the distance between the places as the crow flies. Some researchers use 'born in another county' as a category for analyses such as this. Be aware, if you do this, that places near to county boundaries will have a disproportionate number of out of county in-migrants. County boundaries rarely held significance for our predecessors, so raw distances may be more meaningful.

Sometimes there will be birthplaces that you fail to identify, often because the enumerator has mangled them in some way. You could try identifying this individual in another census, hoping that their place of birth is more comprehensible at that point. Another difficulty is that people can be inconsistent about where they were born. You will have to make a judgement about how you handle these instances, should you be aware of them. Providing you treat all such cases in the same way, your research will retain its validity.

This project can be repeated for other years, to see if the migration patterns change. For a more detailed analysis of in-migration, trace migrants on an individual basis, so that you are aware of the steps in their migration from birthplace to your place. Look at what is going on in your community and in the neighbourhood from which your in-migrants have come. Can you identify any possible reasons for their moves? You can further refine your investigation by considering such things as the age, marital status or occupation of the migrants. You may wish to produce maps to illustrate some of your migrants' journeys.

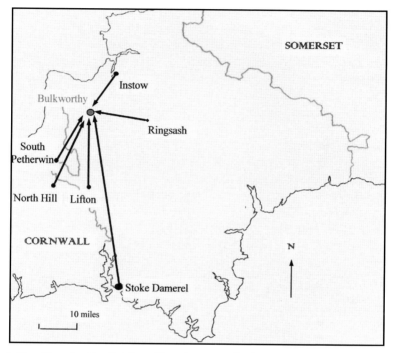

A Map Showing the Origins of In-migrants, who have travelled further than 15 miles to Bulkworthy, Devon 1841-1901

With the availability of online census indexes, many of which allow for birthplace searches, it is comparatively straightforward to find those who have left your community for a destination within Britain. For example, the advanced census search on Ancestry **www.ancestry.co.uk** allows for the entering of a birthplace, without any other information being added to the various search boxes. Do change the default setting to 'restrict to this place exactly', or you will end up with many irrelevant entries. FindmyPast **www.findmypast.co.uk** will permit a search, of all censuses except 1871,[49] by entering your community's name under birthplace. If your place is large,

49 At the time of writing, birthplaces in the 1871 census can only be searched at county level using FindmyPast.

your search may be timed out so enter, in turn, A*, B*, C* etc. under surname until all out-migrants are located. This is also necessary when searching the 1911 census by birthplace on FindmyPast. As with researching in-migration, a clearer picture is gained if you try to follow all the steps taken by each out-migrant.

What these research techniques will not reveal, are those who have left your community for places overseas. These are much more difficult to trace and really need investigating on an individual basis. If you are unable to find a former resident elsewhere in the country, or in the death or burial records, then you may suspect that you have an emigrant. From 1890 onwards, you can check the outward passenger lists. The originals are at The National Archives in Class BT27 and they are available on some subscription websites. These lists only record those leaving Britain for a port outside Europe, so if the boat stopped in France or Spain on the way, a passenger list may not be available. It is possible to check overseas records, such as the Canadian or US census returns but these will give nothing more precise than 'England' as a birthplace. It is difficult to identify people with common surnames in this way. This is another reason why it is helpful to network with those whose ancestors came from your place, as a number of these will be descendants of emigrant inhabitants.

If your place is not a parish or town, it is not possible to research out-migrants in the same way. If, for example, you are studying a single street, people will not give this as their birthplace. It is still feasible to look at out-migration. First you have to identify those who are no longer in your road but do not appear to have died. You then have to follow them up on an individual basis. If there is a place with the same name as your community somewhere overseas, it is worth investigating why this might be. Emigrants from your place may have been early settlers there.

Mapping software is useful when studying migration and has other applications for One Place Studies too. For British maps, Genmap, produced by Archer Software **www.archersoftware.co.uk**, suits the needs of most One Place Studies.

Project - Emigrants

Compile a list of all those you identify as having left your place for an overseas destination. You will have to decide whether or not to include those that you know lived in another place in the UK between their time in your place and their emigration. To make your project more manageable, you may wish to put a terminal date on your list, such as 1914 or 1939. You will also need to decide how much information to collect on each emigrant. The following are suggestions:

Name	Address in your place
Destination	Date of emigration
Name of ship	Date of birth (or age at emigration)
Emigration companions	Occupation (both before and after emigration)

With the inclination, opportunity and a degree of luck, it may be possible to build up fuller biographies of your emigrants. The co-operation of their descendants can be very helpful in this respect. Newspapers for the most popular English speaking destinations are increasingly available online and can be searched for your emigrant, or potential emigrant. These newspapers often carry much fuller obituaries than you might expect to find for someone of the equivalent social status in Britain. For example, the American obituary for John Pennington, who emigrated in 1854 and died in 1942, at the age of ninety six, gave the following information:- his home in the UK (mis-spelt but recognisable), his birthplace and date, his parents' names, details of his emigration, his marriage, his children and grandchildren. There was even a photograph of John.

As with internal migrants, it is interesting to look for motivations for emigration. What was happening in the lives of these emigrants and what was taking place in their former communities, or at their destinations, that might have prompted their move?

Trades, Occupations and Industries

The predominant trades in your community help to give it its unique character. Census reports give broad figures, such as the numbers employed in agriculture or manufacturing however the census returns and directories are often the best sources for a more detailed analysis. Paul Glennie's *Distinguishing Men's Trades: occupational sources and debates for pre-census England* (University of Bristol 1990) suggests some pre census sources for researching trades and occupations; these include militia lists, tax lists, probate records and parish registers. Dennis R Mills' *Rural Community History from Trade Directories* (Local Population Studies 2001) is also useful, providing ideas for studying occupations.

Project - Occupational Structure

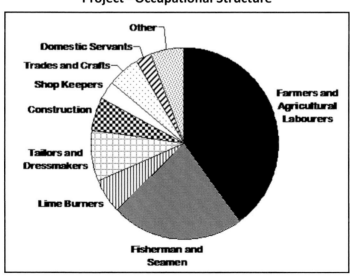

Occupational Structure in Bucks Mills in 1841.

You need to use a fairly comprehensive list of all the occupations in your place at a specific date. This usually means that you will be working from a census return or directory. Calculate how many individuals are following each occupation. It is likely that you will have to group the occupations into categories, in order not to make your list too unwieldy. For example, tailors, milliners and dressmakers could be treated as a single occupation. Butchers, grocers and bakers could all be classified as 'shopkeepers'. You can also use the census returns of 1891-1911 to analyse how many of your residents were employers, employees or self employed. It may be that your findings will vary in different parts of your place.

Part of your study might involve tracing the history of a particular source of employment in your place. This could be a mill, mine, factory or a home industry such as straw plaiting or glovemaking. If you are researching the history of a company or industrial enterprise, they may have their own archive. Check at your local record office and with the National Register of Archives.[50] Can you associate named residents of your community with this business? You may wish to consider tools used, working conditions, clothing worn and wages paid. Do not neglect agriculture as a source of employment. Farms and farming are a key element of many places and some projects relating to farms have already been suggested.[51] It is interesting to investigate such things as types of agriculture, sizes of farms and number of employees.

Services, Institutions and Societies

The old adage that a church, a school and a pub make a community is not far wrong. Other institutions, such as a workhouse, a hospital, non-conformist chapels or a railway station, may be features of your location. More recent amenities might include playing fields, art galleries, museums, sports centres, libraries, parks and allotments. These are all part of the fabric of your place and worthy of investigation. When researching the history of workhouses, the best starting point is Peter Higginbotham's excellent website **www.workhouses.org.uk**. He has written several books on the subject including *The Workhouse Encyclopaedia* (The History Press 2012). The Pub History Society website **www.pubhistorysociety.co.uk** is useful. If you are researching a pub, it is a good idea to check for Victuallers' Licenses, which are to be found with Quarter Sessions records[52] in County Record Offices. Directories and newspapers[53] are also helpful.

Other possible research topics are the various clubs, societies and leisure opportunities that have been available in the area over the years. Most places have high days, holidays and festivities. Some are regular activities; others, such as VE day celebrations, are a one-off. You might wish to research fetes, markets, harvest festivals, jubilees, Sunday school treats and similar celebrations.

---

[50] See Chapter 4, p. 26. [51] See Chapters 5, p. 38 and 6, p. 42.

[52] See Chapter 7, p. 54. [53] See Chapters 5, p. 33 and 6, p. 45.

Historically, leisure activities and clubs were often associated with the church or chapel, more recently, they have become increasingly diverse. If you decide to study the history of a local club, an opportunity for collaboration might arise. For example, could you enlist the help of current members of the Young Farmers' Club, the Women's Institute or Football Club, to help you research the history of their society? Newspapers[54] are an excellent source of relevant information. Try searching online newspapers for your place name AND 'club', 'society' or 'institute'.

Charities can also be researched. Again these were often associated with the church, who might be appointed trustees when a legacy needed administering for charitable purposes. In the era before the welfare state, friendly societies or mutual insurance clubs, such the Rechabites or the Foresters were common. Societies that may help with such research include the Voluntary Action History Society, which promotes the history of charitable organisations and voluntary action **www. vahs.org.uk** and The Friendly Societies Research Group **www.open.ac.uk/ socialsciences/friendly-societies-research-group**.

Project - Services

Examine the services in your community at a particular point in time. This can include different types of shops, associations and other facilities. You might include the institutions, services and societies mentioned above. Directories are a good source for this project but you may have to supplement the information with such things as newspapers and census returns. Did your community have a chapel, a doctor, a literary society, a railway or a baker's shop? Just how self-sufficient would your place have been at that date? You will probably find significant changes if you repeat this exercise for a different time. Whilst the facilities in urban areas tend to become more diverse, those in rural communities are more likely to dwindle.

The research projects in this and earlier, chapters become all the more meaningful if you can evaluate your findings alongside those for other communities. The Family and Community Historical Research Society **www.fachrs.com** encourage their members to collaborate and undertake similar projects, so that the results can then be compared. Many members of the Society for One-Place Studies **one-place-studies.org** undertake projects similar to those in this book, sometimes as group undertakings. It may be that you can find someone who has already studied their place in a similar way so that your own community can be set in a broader context.

Further Reading
Adolph, Anthony *Tracing your Home's History* (Harper Collins 2006).
Barrett, Nick *Tracing the History of your House* (The National Archives 2006).
Brooks, Pamela *How to Research your House: every home tells a story* (Howtobooks 2007), this contains a particularly good section on architectural styles.

---

[54] See Chapter 6, p. 45.

Clark, Peter *British Clubs and Societies 1580-1800: the origins of an associational world* (Clarendon Press 2000).

Glennie, Paul *Distinguishing Men's Trades: occupational sources and debates for pre-census England* (University of Bristol 1990).

Haydon, Peter *The English Pub: a history* (Robert Hale 1994).

Higginbotham, Peter *The Workhouse Encyclopaedia* (The History Press 2012).

Mills, Dennis R *Rural Community History from Trade Directories* (Local Population Studies 2001).

Myerson, Julie *Home: the story of everyone who ever lived in our house* (Harper Perennial 2005), an interesting individual house history, together with an account of the research trail.

Risse, G *Mending Bodies, Saving Souls: a history of hospitals* (Oxford University Press 1999).

Chapter 12

Publicising and Disseminating your One Place Study

Marketing your One Place Study

Publicising your One Place Study enables others, who may have valuable details about your community and its inhabitants, to get in touch. So it is important that your research and contact details are widely advertised. Some methods of doing so will require a membership fee or payment, other options will be free. Some opportunities are only available to groups, rather than individuals. You should certainly publicise your One Place Study with the relevant county, or district, Family History Society. As mentioned in Chapter Eleven, members' interests lists may be searchable by place, enabling you to exchange information with those researching families who resided in your community. Have you asked your local church(es) if your research and contact details can be displayed by their visitors' book? Many ancestor hunters visit the local church and record their interests. If you are not able to advertise, then it is a good idea to search through the visitors' book as often as you can to see if anyone has expressed an interest in a particular family or building.

Do not restrict yourself to the family or local history world. Make sure your research is marketed locally, on parish websites or in village newsletters. Any major developments or events related to your One Place Study may warrant contacting the local media and result in some publicity. An article in the local paper is far more likely to be read than an advertisement and has the added advantage of being free. Your One Place Study is also brought to the wider world through your 'publications'; see 'Publishing your One Place Study' below.

The following are worth considering as methods of promoting your work:
The Society for One-Place Studies **one-place-studies.org**
The Register of One Place Studies **www.register-of-one-place-studies.org.uk**
The Community Archives and Heritage Group **www.communityarchives.org.uk**
British Association for Local History **www.balh.co.uk**.
Local History Online **www.local-history.co.uk/index.html**.
Genuki **www.genuki.org.uk**. Your One Place Study should appear on the relevant parish page, even if you aren't an Online Parish Clerk.
Robert and Elizabeth Blatchford's *Family and Local History Handbook* (Robert Blatchford Publishing Ltd. issued periodically) **www.genealogical.co.uk**.

Funding your One Place Study

The majority of One Place Studies, particularly those that are the work of individual researchers, are entirely self-funded. It is virtually impossible to generate an income from a One Place Study but it should be possible to find ways of offsetting some of the costs of the research. There may be times when seeking financial support might be appropriate; for example, in order to mount a display or publish a book. It is often the first project that is the hardest to fund. Once you have a publication to sell or have raised money from holding an open day, you have a small pot of money for your next venture.

If you have been going it alone so far, the need for funding may prompt the formation of a group. This provides the opportunity of collecting membership fees, although clearly you have to have something to offer members in return. In this way you acquire a group of potential fund raisers as well as an audience for any product or event that you may create. You may be able to persuade individuals to contribute to the purchase of copies of a particular class of documents. For example, during the activities that accompanied the centenary of the outbreak of the First World War, one community held a meeting to share the results of research into those on the local war memorial. Attendees at that meeting were invited to sponsor the purchase of copies of Soldiers' Wills (see **probatesearch.service.gov.uk/**) for their community, at a cost of £6 a time. Another option would have been to have had a raffle at that event for the same purpose.

It is worth exploring the possibility of Heritage Lottery Funding (HLF), as well as local grant options, such as parish council awards or loans. There are various groups, including HLF itself, who can offer advice, notably The Community Archives and Heritage Group **www.communityarchives.org.uk**. Grants can often come from unexpected places. If your place is in an Area of Outstanding Natural Beauty, AONB **www.aonb.org.uk** might agree to support a project that enhances awareness of the landscape as well as the built heritage.

The Future of your One Place Study

The best way to ensure that your research survives and is enhanced after you are no longer able to be its custodian, is to involve other people, ideally young people. This does not mean the newly retired, this means children. There is not space in this book to go into precise details of how to inspire and interest the under eighteens but it can and should be done. Several of the projects in this volume mention their appropriateness for involving young people and it is well worth any extra work this might make.

Can you enlist your own children, grandchildren, nieces or nephews to assist with research? It is more difficult if they do not live near you but not impossible, especially with free internet communications such as Skype **www.skype.com** or Google+ **plus.google.com**. What about the local school, youth group, scout or guide association? Child protection policies mean that those associating with children in these settings need stringent safeguarding checks, so be prepared for this. Whether or not you have to undergo such checks will depend on exactly how you will be working with the young people.

Not everyone has a rapport with children. If you feel you do not have the necessary skills, work with someone who does. It is vital that we play a role in fostering a love of history in the next generation. The ideal way of doing so is through something personal, such as the history of their locality.

It is a good idea to make arrangements for the preservation and ideally continuation, of your study in the event of your being unable to do so yourself. This may mean passing it on to a successor or lodging it with a society or record office. Do make sure that your nearest and dearest know what your intentions are, that all the necessary passwords or log in details are passed on and that your chosen recipient is willing to receive the fruits of your labours. This issue is dealt with in detail in Alex Coles' article *Till Death Us Do Part — Estate Planning for your OPS* (2012) accessible via **one-place-studies.org/articles/til-death-us-do-part-estate-planning-for-your-ops/**.

Publishing your One Place Study

Anyone undertaking a One Place Study should aim to make it available to others in some form. Not only does this give the work a focus and purpose but 'publishing' aspects of your research will frequently lead to additional material coming your way. For some, a single 'end product' publication will suit. Others will want to make their findings accessible in stages, or in a way that can be added to or updated. There is no right or wrong way to go about this. Often a combination of methods will be the most appropriate. All the possibilities have both advantages and drawbacks. Some of these are outlined below, so that each researcher can decide what best meets their needs.

The word 'publish' usually brings print and paper to mind. A book certainly looks impressive and may be a good way in which to tell a complete story. It is also a considerable undertaking, particularly if you are working alone. Books, especially those with plentiful illustrations and small print runs, can be expensive to produce. You are very unlikely to attract a commercial publisher who will finance your project, although grant funding of some kind might be a possibility. You may be able to persuade potential purchasers to part with cash up front, in return for a favourable pre-publication price. Another disadvantage of a book is that it tends to be a one off enterprise. What will happen to the information that you gather after publication? Some of these difficulties can be solved if you opt for an ebook, or convert your text to a pdf and distribute it by email or on a CD. It is much easier to revise a digital book. There will still be a large proportion of your potential audience however who will not be comfortable with a digital format. The commercial firm, Lulu Publishing **www.lulu.com**, produce printed books on a one off basis, allowing for updating at any stage. They print to order, with the cost being met by individual purchasers. Another option is Smashwords **www.smashwords.com**.

There is no legal requirement to do so but many book publishers decide to apply for International Standard Book Numbers (ISBNs); see **www.isbn.nielsenbook. co.uk**. Booksellers and libraries use ISBNs to catalogue and order publications. Some sellers will not market a publication that does not have an ISBN. The initial cost of a series of ISBNs is not inconsiderable and copies of each publication have to be sent to the copyright libraries. For this reason, unless you are planning a prolific and profitable publications output, you may decide not to bother.

Although it may not look as imposing, a series of booklets is often preferable to a book. Several articles on different topics, produced in turn, is effectively publishing your book a chapter at a time. This is much more easily attainable and reduces the initial financial outlay. The booklets could be collated to form a book at a later date. It also makes multi-authorship more straightforward. In addition, this approach may allow you to create articles that will be acceptable to journal or magazine editors. The downside is that each booklet only tells part of the story of your place.

Especially if your One Place Study is a group enterprise, you may produce a regular newsletter. This allows for recent developments to be reported and more substantial articles to be published. If you do produce a newsletter it is a good idea to apply for an International Standard Serial Number or ISSN. You need separate ISSNs for paper and digital serial publications. There is no charge for an ISSN. Details of how to apply can be found on the website **www.issn.org**. Books, booklets and newsletters can all be circulated in digital or paper form. Whilst digital publications have huge financial benefits, the advantage of a paper based publication is that the format is not likely to become obsolete or unreadable in the foreseeable future.

You may decide to disseminate your One Place Study via a website. People often worry about the expertise required to create a website but it can be comparatively straightforward. The most difficult part is usually creating the content, which you will need to do whatever your chosen method of publication. There may be a cost implication but free webspace options are usually sufficient for all but the most extensive One Place Studies. The obvious advantages of a website are that it is easy to update and that you can add links to other relevant websites. Compared to printed options, a website is likely to bring your research within reach of an audience with a rather different demographic. This can only benefit the longevity of your research. If your website is your only method of disseminating your One Place Study, you need to be aware that it may not survive for long if you are no longer able to fund or maintain the site. This is less of a problem if you are researching as part of a group, who will hopefully see that the data migrates to new forms of technology, that at present we can only imagine.

If you do not feel you want to set up your own website, there are sites that encourage you to upload One Place Study information. The Society for One-Place Studies allocates members the space to display a short description as well as 'In Depth' material, including some illustrations. Other options include Ehive **ehive.com**, Share History **sharehistory.org/**, Treflix **www.treflix.com** and My.parish.org **my-**

parish.org. Some counties also have facilities to upload data relating to local history such as Devon Heritage **www.devonheritage.org**.

Blogs can stand alone or form a part of a more static website. There is no doubt that a blog, if used regularly, brings traffic to your website and helps it to rise up the rankings of the various search engines. A blog is effectively a journal, or a way of sharing the latest developments and news of your One Place Study. There are millions of blogs on the world wide web and only the most dedicated of fellow researchers are likely to follow your blog assiduously. Nevertheless, whilst it may not be suitable as the only method of publishing your One Place Study, a blog can be a very useful way of advertising your research and letting interested parties know what is going on.

Another way in which aspects of your One Place Study might be made public is by video. This is particularly suited to broadcasting oral history; it is highly pictorial and popular with a wide potential audience. The necessary equipment requires financial outlay but after that, it is cheap to create and easy to distribute. This is a format that may go out of date very quickly and unless the technology is continually transferred, your video may be unwatchable within a fairly short space of time. If the finished product is to be of a reasonable quality, some technical expertise is required.

Increasingly, YouTube clips or podcasts are watched by people of all ages and might be a way of publishing an aspect of your One Place Study. See for example, *Yapton: a Sussex parish seen through the census and parish records*, a 50 minute talk from Tony Wakeford that is available via The National Archive website **http://media.nationalarchives.gov.uk/index.php/yapton-a-sussex-parish-seen-through-the-census-and-parish-records/**.

Presentations or talks about aspects of your research are good ways to spread the word. Power point presentations are highly visual, can be altered easily and are cheaply and simply distributed to those who cannot be present at a lecture. Without a narrator however the presentation may need accompanying text, if it is to be understood. This is another format that may go out of date rapidly. Regular exhibitions or displays will help to interest others in your work. It a good idea to combine exhibitions or talks with the suggestion that the audience bring photographs or memorabilia with them to share. Consider having a stand at a family or local history fair. This is an alternative if you do not want to hold an open day of your own. You are more likely to raise funds by staging your own event. Attendance at a fair run by someone else may well require you to pay a stand fee. You will have to have plenty to sell to recoup the costs of this but you may view it as being well worth it for the publicity alone. Good quality displays are not cheap to produce. Ensure the longevity of your display materials by omitting such things as contact details, which may change. These can be provided on more cheaply produced handouts or cards.

You should not be reluctant to use social media for serious research, or underestimate its potential. A Facebook page or group **www.facebook.com** or a Twitter feed **twitter.com** may play an important part in spreading news of the latest developments in your research. Social networking is defined as 'a way of using online

resources and services to create and maintain a community of individuals who share a common interest'.[55] If you were offered a way of freely maintaining a community of individuals who shared an interest in your One Place Study, would you turn it down? If you are at all sceptical about this, watch this short video **youtu.be/3SuNxo UrnEo**. For now, a quote by Eric Qualman from that video:- 'We don't have a choice on whether we do social media - the question is how well we do it'. I am a little less dogmatic. I perfectly respect anyone's wish not to use social media themselves. If however this is you, be aware that you are missing a valuable, if not essential, tool and you may do well to consider getting someone to social network on your behalf. This could be the ideal opportunity to involve the next generation in your research.

What do I Say?

It is no good planning to distribute your research via a particular medium unless you have something to share. Some people find this the most difficult aspect of conducting their One Place Study. If you sit down to write about your place you may well end up staring at a blank sheet of paper or a computer screen. As with any piece of writing, what makes it easier is dividing it in to sections and tackling one at a time. Looking at the work of others is invaluable. You can then decide what works and what approaches you wish to avoid. Any or all of the topics below might be of interest and there will be others that you can add. A selection from these headings could form the chapters of a book, articles for a blog or pages on a website. If you are struggling to make a start, chose the subjects that you feel are most relevant to your One Place Study and commit to getting to grips with one a week, or one a month, or what ever deadline suits you. Realistic deadlines are important. It is all too easy to keep letting 'writing it up' slip to the bottom of the 'to do' pile.

---

[55] Smith, Drew *Social Networking for Genealogists* (Genealogical Publishing Company 2009).

Situation - where is your 'place'? Is it, for example, rural, coastal or a street in market town?

Geography - describe the terrain, soil and rivers.

Route ways - how might people have arrived in your place at different times in history? Describe roads, railways, carriers, river and sea routes.

Population - how many people lived in your place at various dates? Describe any fluctuations and possible reasons for these. What was the age/sex structure at different times?

Kinship Links - how dense are these at various times?

Migration - analyse in and out-migration. Where did people come from and go to?

Buildings - both residential and non-residential. Think about when they were built, their construction and size. Describe any notable buildings.

Historical Events - construct a timeline of significant occurrences in your place.

Occupations - describe the predominant occupations and industries in your place and any changes in these over time.

Social Structure - analyse the class profile of your place at particular times.

Agriculture - if applicable, describe farming types, the number and size of farms in your place.

Worship - describe the churches, chapels, synagogues, temples and other places of worship in your place. What impact have various denominations and faiths had on your community in the past?

Education - schools and school teachers.

Shops and Services - how did these change over time?

Clubs and Societies.

High Days and Holidays - include one-off celebrations, regular fairs, markets and other events.

Predominant 'dynastic' surnames in the area.
Residential Persistence - how long did individuals and families remain in your place?
Notable Residents - biographies of any well known former residents.

Project - Timeline

Create a timeline for the history of your place, incorporating all the significant events that you discover whilst researching various themes for your One Place Study. You might include such things as:

The total population at specific dates.
The building, extending or closure of places of worship.
The arrival, or demise of railways, canals or other transport links.
The opening of schools.
The construction of prominent buildings or groups of houses.
The granting of charters for fairs or markets.
The birth or death of prominent residents.
Fires, floods and extreme weather events.

A One Place Study is what you make it. As long as the research techniques are sound, there is no right and wrong way of going about your work. This intensely personal brand of history is a wonderful way of encouraging others to engage with their heritage. So it only remains for me to say, enjoy investigating and sharing the history of your place. Your perceptions of the past and indeed your life, may never be the same again.

Some Examples of One Place Study Websites

Auchindrain, Argyll, Scotland **auchindrain.wikidot.com/**
Coldingham, Berwickshire, Scotland **vivdunstan.co.uk/coldingham-ops.html**
Wing, Buckinghamshire **www.wing-ops.org.uk**
Stanley, Derbyshire **freepages.genealogy.rootsweb.ancestry.com/**
  ~alanbloor/SOPS.htm
Buckland Brewer, Devon - including a blog **bucklandbrewerhistorygroup.**
  wordpress.com
Hartland, Devon **www.hartlandforum.co.uk**
'Beyond the Point' South East Essex **beyondthepoint.co.uk/**
Brooke, Isle of Wight **www.brookvillagehistory.co.uk/**
Springhill, Rossendale, Lancashire **springhillhistory.org.uk**
High Littleton and Hallatrow, Somerset **www.highlittletonhistory.org.uk/**
Parham, Suffolk Facebook Page **www.facebook.com/pages/Parham-**
  Suffolk/1414553592093177?ref=hl
Bubwith, East Yorkshire **www.bubwith.net**

Bibliography

Adolph, Anthony *Collins' Tracing Your Family History* (Collins 2008).
Barrett, Nick *Beginners' Guide to Family History* (Pen and Sword 2010).
Bristow, Joy *The Local Historian's Glossary of Words and Terms* (Countryside Books 2001).
Brooks, Pamela *How to Research Local History* (How to Books 2006).
Cole, Jean and Titford, John *Tracing your Family Tree* (Countryside Books 2000).
Coles, Alex, *Til Death Us Do Part — Estate Planning for your OPS* (2012) http://one-place-studies.org/articles/til-death-us-do-part-estate-planning-for-your-ops/.
Drake, Michael *Time, Family and Community* (Blackwells 1994).
Drake, Michael and Finnegan, Ruth *Sources and Methods for Family and Community History: a handbook* (Cambridge University Press 1994).
Dymond, David *Researching and Writing History: a guide for local historians* (Carnegie Publishing Ltd. 2009).
Everitt, Alan M *Landscape and Community in England* (Hambledon Continuum 1985).
Few, Janet (ed.) *Family Historians' Enquire Within* (Family History Partnership 2014).
Fowler, Simon *Family History: digging deeper* (The History Press 2012).
Fowler, Simon *Starting out in Local History* (Countryside Books 2001).
Friar, Stephen *The Local History Companion* (The History Press 2001).
Girouard, Mark *The English Town* (Yale UP 1990).

Golby, John *Communities and Families* (Cambridge University Press 1994).

Hawgood, David *One-Place Genealogy* (David Hawgood 2001).

Hey, David *Family History and Local History in England* (Longman 1987).

Hey, David *The Oxford Companion to Local and Family History* (2nd edition Oxford University Press 2010).

Hoskins, W G *The Midland Peasant: the economic and social history of a Leicestershire village* (Phillimore 2008).

Hoskins, W G and Boyd, William *The Making of the English Landscape* (Little Toller Books 2013).

Hoskins, W G and Hey, David *Local History in England* (Longmans 1984).

Iredale, David and Barrett, John *Discovering Local History* (Shire Publications 1999).

Laslett, Peter *The World we have Lost: further explained* (4th edition Routledge 2005).

Martin, C T *The Record Interpreter: a collection of abbreviations, Latin words and names used in English historical manuscripts and records* (reprinted Forgotten Books 2012).

Miller, E and Hatcher J *Medieval England: rural society and economic change 1086-1348* (Longman 1978).

Mills, David *A Dictionary of British Place Names* (revised edition OUP 2011).

Mills, Dennis R *The English Village* (Routledge and Kegan Paul 1968).

Morton, Ann and Donaldson, Gordon *British National Archives and the Local Historian* (The Historical Association 1981).

Porter, Stephen *Exploring Urban History: sources for local historians* (Batsford Ltd. 1991).

Pryce, W T R *From Family History to Community History* (Cambridge University Press 1994).

Pryor, Francis *The Making of the British Landscape: how we have transformed the land, from prehistory to today* (Penguin 2011).

Reay, Barry *Microhistories: demography, society and culture in rural England, 1800-1930* (Cambridge, 1996).

Reay, Barry *Rural Englands* (Palgrave Macmillan 2004).

Richardson, John *The Local Historian's Encyclopedia* (3rd edition Historical Publications Ltd. 2003).

Riden, Philip *Local History: a handbook for beginners* (2nd edition Merton Priory Press 1998).

Riden, Philip *Record Sources for Local History* (Batsford 1987).

Stephens, W B *Sources for English Local History* (revised edition Cambridge University Press 1981).

Tate, W E *The Parish Chest* (3rd edition Phillimore 2010).

Tiller, Kate *English Local History: an introduction* (Alan Sutton 1992).

West, John *Town Records* (Phillimore 1983).

West, John *Village Records* (Phillimore 1997).

Williams, Michael A *Researching Local History: the human journey* (Longman 1996).
Wood, Michael *The Story of England* (Viking 2010)
Yorke, Trevor *The English Village Explained* (Countryside Books 2011).

National Archives Research Guides, that are referred to in this volume, can be accessed by going to www.nationalarchives.gov.uk, 'Records', 'Find Guidance' and then the appropriate letter of the alphabet.

Magazines and Journals

The are also some useful magazines and journals including:
Destinations **one-place-studies.org**
Local History Magazine **www.local-history.co.uk**
The Local Historian and *Local History News* **www.balh.co.uk**
Local Population Studies **www.localpopulationstudies.org.uk**
Family and Community History **www.fachrs.com**
Oral History **www.oralhistory.org.uk**

Societies and Websites

Society for One-Place Studies **one-place-studies.org**
The Family and Community History Research Society **www.fachrs.com**
British Association for Local History **www.balh.co.uk**
Community Archives and Heritage Group **www.communityarchives.org.uk**
The Oral History Society **www.oralhistory.org.uk**
English Place Name Society **www.nottingham.ac.uk/ins/placenamesociety/ index.aspx**
Local Population Studies Society **www.localpopulationstudies.org.uk**
The Cambridge Group for the History of Population and Social Structure
www.geog.cam.ac.uk/research/centres/campop/
Scottish Local History Forum **www.slhf.org**
Local History Online **www.local-history.co.uk**
Urban History Resources Hub **www2.le.ac.uk/departments/urbanhistory/ resources/uh-hub**
The Centre for English Local History **www.le.ac.uk/elh/**
Museum of English Rural Life **www.reading.ac.uk/merl/**
National Museum of Rural Life (Scotland) **www.nms.ac.uk/our_museums/ museum_of_rural_life.aspx**
The Historical Association **www.history.org.uk**
History.Uk.com **www.history.uk.com**
The Institute of Historical Research **www.history.ac.uk**
The Royal Historical Society **www.royalhistoricalsociety.org**
The Bibliography of British and Irish History
www.history.ac.uk/projects/bbih

Courses

There are a number of extra mural, correspondence and online courses that are relevant to One Place Studies. See **www.local-history.co.uk/Courses/** for a list of, mostly university based, courses, some of which require attendance in person. There are also courses run by local adult education providers, the Workers' Education Association **www.wea.org.uk** and Family History Societies, which tend to be shorter, cheaper and lacking in assignments. Please note that URLs for courses go out of date very quickly. If those below no longer work, it is worth enquiring of the relevant institution to see if they are still offering the course, or something similar.

The following are just a selection:
National Institute for Genealogical Studies Organizing a One-Place Study
www.genealogicalstudies.com
Pharos One-Place Studies: research from a new perspective
www.pharostutors.com/coursesmainsd.php
University of Birmingham MA in West Midlands' History **www.birmingham. ac.uk/postgraduate/courses/taught/history/west-midlands-history.aspx**
University of Dundee Postgraduate Certificate in Family and Local History
www.dundee.ac.uk/cais/certificate
University of Exeter Village and Parish History: Reconstructing the Local Past, 1500-1800 **http://education.exeter.ac.uk/dll/details.php?code=DLH12** and Parish to Community History: Researching the Local Past, 1800-2000 **http://education.exeter.ac.uk/dll/details.php?code=DLH13**
University of Hull offer a Certificate, Diploma and BA in Regional and Local History
www2.hull.ac.uk/FASS/history__hull/regional-local_history.aspx
Keele University Certificate in Local History
www.keele.ac.uk/hums/shortcoursesandcontinuingeducation
Lancaster University Postgraduate Certificate in Regional and Local History: Sources and Approaches **www.lancs.ac.uk/fass/history/postgrad/ pgcertificate.htm**
University of Leicester MA in English Local History **www2.le.ac.uk/ departments/history/postgraduate/taught/englishlocal**
University of London, Institute of Historical Research MA in Historical Research
www.history.ac.uk/study/ma
University of Oxford Undergraduate Advanced Diploma in Local History
www.conted.ox.ac.uk/courses/details.php?id=30
University of Roehampton MA or Postgraduate Diploma in Historical Research
www.roehampton.ac.uk/postgraduate-courses/historical-research/index.html

Index